GW01311660

B2B

SOCIAL MEDIA

The Complete Guide to Developing
a B2B Social Media Strategy
(Plus a Case Study)

Rich Walker

Published by Digitally Rich

ISBN-13: 978-1523605309
ISBN-10: 1523605308

CONTENTS

PREFACE

Before I became interested in digital marketing, a good friend of mine suggested that I try my hand at content writing. A failed high school English class and less than modest writing experience made it seem unlikely this path would open up for me. And yet, an international tech company struggling to find a content writer gave me my big break. Working in that marketing department was a buzz I had never experienced before as an IT specialist. It drove me to learn all I could about content marketing, which led me to study SEO, which led me to study online advertising, which led me to study social media, which led me to where I am now; working mainly with B2B companies but also with customer-facing clients as a consultant.

There are so many great resources on developing a social

media strategy to boost brand awareness and increase sales. But it shocked me to discover how little information is available for B2B companies trying to enhance their social media presence and generate qualified leads.

The aim of this book, therefore, is to bring together my experiences of developing a B2B social media strategy—many times learning through failure—and assist you in determining the optimal use of social media for your B2B business. By applying several different expert perspectives from industry thought leaders, internet marketing geeks, savvy social media strategists, top business speakers and consultants, and all-round digital media influencers in real-world working environments, I have discovered what works and can now bring this knowledge to you.

That's not to say that my total strategy will remain valid forever. Rather, I believe at least 90% of the tactics and tools I explain in this book will be applicable, indeed, valuable for any business or individual looking to achieve their objectives on social media for the foreseeable future. The other 10% is open to improvements to the strategy and any necessary modifications to keep up with upgrades to social media platforms.

Who This Book is For

I wanted to write this book not only to help B2B businesses get on social media but also to include strategies that can be easily adapted for brands in the business-to-consumer field aiming to drive sales through social media. I thought it essential, then, that it contained uncomplicated information about how to make the most of the top social media platforms, how to manage social media content creation and posting, how to target your audience, how to find the right people to follow, and how to engage with fans, followers, and equally important, non-followers. As a result, I hope this book lets you take control of your social media marketing efforts and reach your goals whether they be lead generation or customer acquisition.

How This Book is Structured

I split this book into four parts; the first three tackling a different aspect of my social media strategy for B2B companies and the final part showing you how the previous three parts work in a real-world environment. Now, I don't expect you to read each chapter in turn so feel free to skip to any and all relevant chapters but this book has been laid out in a sort of timeline as I see your strategy developing. That means if you are already past selecting your social media platform selection process and have set up your branded profiles, for example, you can move directly to Part II. In a nutshell, this book is set out in the aforementioned logical steps as follows:

- Part I examines why social media is important for B2B companies and investigates which popular social media platforms are most relevant and beneficial.

- Part II examines which social media management tools can streamline and simplify ongoing social media content development after deciding on the type of content you will create.

- Part III discusses how social media activity should be monitored and reported, in addition to listing the best practices of social media marketing on LinkedIn, Facebook, and Twitter.

- Part IV then details the development of a social media strategy designed to introduce a B2B company to the online world, increase their social presence, and begin to generate targeted leads.

More specifically, Chapters 10 and 11 present a case study. The primary source of field research came from a small Australian ad agency specialising in brand design and development. At present, the agency acquires clients via referrals and word of mouth, with little to no marketing on or offline. You will read how I managed to optimise their social media activity based on their limited resources so that the CEO (the individual responsible for managing branded social media profiles) can perform the necessary tasks in just 15 minutes a day.

The book closes with a reflection on the entire strategy outlined from Chapter 1 through to Chapter 9, including the complete social media checklist, and offers a few recommendations for future social media and internet marketing activity.

Terms Used and Special Sections

Throughout the book, I use terms such as social media associate, specialist or team. I understand that you, an employee, an intern, a virtual assistant, your tech-savvy teenage offspring, etc. will manage your social media efforts. Please accept any of these terms to mean the actual person or people in charge of your social media profiles. That includes content creation, user engagement, and performance tracking. If you need clarification on other terms used in this book, flip to the glossary at the back for a brief definition.

Action steps conclude Chapters 1 through 9. They are designed to help you first launch your foray into social media and then make sure it continues with focussed effort. You may check off these action steps as you reach them or go through the entire book and understand each section before completing the full checklist given at the end of Chapter 12.

The action step checklist is not the only resource you will use in your own strategy. Other tools recommended throughout this book offer further assistance in boosting your lead generation endeavours via consistent actions. These tools are the actual ones I use when advising companies on their social media strategies and offer advice on how to create them.

Wherever possible, I have also tried to highlight B2B companies doing great things on social media. Learning from other brands, including your direct competitors, is a simple but valuable exercise in taking your social media strategy performance to the next level. Please do not take it to mean I have any affiliation with any of these companies and I can disclose that I do not make any profit whatsoever from my suggestions. Now that you know what to expect, let's get started!

PART I

Socially Rich B2B

Chapter 1 – Social Media for B2B Companies
Chapter 2 – Social Media Platform Choice
Chapter 3 – Best Practice Guide

Part I serves as an introduction to social media for B2B companies. What's most exciting about social media for B2B is the ease of entry and capacity for generating leads. What's scariest about social media for B2B is getting started and keeping things going once you launch from the starting grid; especially for businesses with little resources to devote to tweeting, pinning, and liking.

The whole process becomes a little easier when you define your objectives for using social media and select the most suitable platforms. To help with this task, Chapter 2 provides a B2B-focussed examination of each of the top eight social media platforms as used by B2B marketers.

Knowing more about popular social media platforms is one thing. Knowing how to use them effectively is quite another. Chapter 3 delves into the best practices for each of the top eight platforms, giving you handy tips on content creation that's less about you and your services and more about the interests of your target audience.

CHAPTER ONE:
SOCIAL MEDIA FOR B2B COMPANIES

Your need for acceptance can make you invisible in this world. Risk being seen in all of your glory.
- JIM CARREY

CHAPTER CONTENTS

- B2B on Social Media
- Social Media Platforms
- Objectives

87% of B2B Marketers Consider This to Be the Most Effective Marketing Tactic – B2B on Social Media

Social media presents considerable marketing opportunities for individuals and small to large businesses. Companies serving business-to-business (B2B) and/or business-to-consumer (B2C) audiences can use social media to promote the brand and the business, tell customers about goods and services, find out what customers think of the business, attract new clients, and build stronger relationships with existing customers and clients. There are no obstacles to entry or financial barriers, and it can provide valuable support to an overarching marketing communication strategy.

Yet despite the ease and zero cost of setting up social media profiles there is a downside. Social media is only a cost-effective marketing strategy in the sense that the platforms are free to use. Maintaining consistent content creation and user interaction demands a significant amount of time and resources allocated to a dedicated social media specialist or team to gain meaningful results. Even knowledgeable marketers find it difficult to justify efforts versus results; particularly when a company's social media intangible objectives include brand awareness and relationship building. To make matters worse, all of this activity occurs in a public space where almost every competitor is also battling for the attention of the same audience. But it's not all doom and gloom. Let's focus on the positives.

Social media has opened the door for two-way interaction, making it more important than ever to listen to and converse with customers. No other communication strategy can give marketers a clearer understanding of a company's target audience, a wider reach for disseminating brand messages and building brand awareness, a better way to minimise marketing expenses while increasing lead generation, or a greater method of building relationships with potential clients without meeting face-to-face. What's more, many of these outcomes can be achieved without even selling anything. In fact, social media etiquette condemns it. With so many benefits, there is little reason for any and all businesses not to have a social presence, right?

Depending on the marketing blog you read, it has been estimated that up to 87% of B2B marketers apply their trade on social media—considering it to be the most effective tactic of all types of content marketing—while 80% plan on increasing the amount of resources allocated to social media in the future. A study of the 100 largest Fortune 500 companies by Deepa and Deshmukh (2013) found that 86 of them have a business profile on social media, with Twitter revealed as the most popular platform amongst this group. Perhaps it's not such a surprising statistic considering the amount of available resources large organisations have at their disposal to allocate to a dedicated in-house or outsourced social media team.

What's most shocking is that 14 of the 100 largest Fortune 500 companies don't have a single social media profile. I've already mentioned Twitter but where else are B2B digital marketers likely to hang out online?

Where Do B2B Digital Marketers Hang Out? – Popular Social Media Platforms

The eight most popular social media sites said to be adopted by B2B digital marketers are LinkedIn[1], Twitter[2], Facebook[3], YouTube[4], Google+[5], SlideShare[6], Pinterest[7], and Instagram[8], with the majority of B2B digital marketers favouring LinkedIn. The chart on the next page presents key statistics of these eight top social media sites from 2014 in terms of total monthly active users globally, monthly active users in Australia, and usage by B2B marketers. It is likely a comparable chart can be made for B2B social media use for any of you that apply your trade in North America, Europe, or elsewhere (just update the black segments to reflect monthly active users in the country of your choice—and hopefully you can find some national user statistics on SlideShare!).

---

[1] http://www.linkedin.com/
[2] http://twitter.com/
[3] http://www.Facebook.com/
[4] http://www.youtube.com/
[5] https://plus.google.com/
[6] http://www.slideshare.net/
[7] http://www.pinterest.com/
[8] http://www.instagram.com/

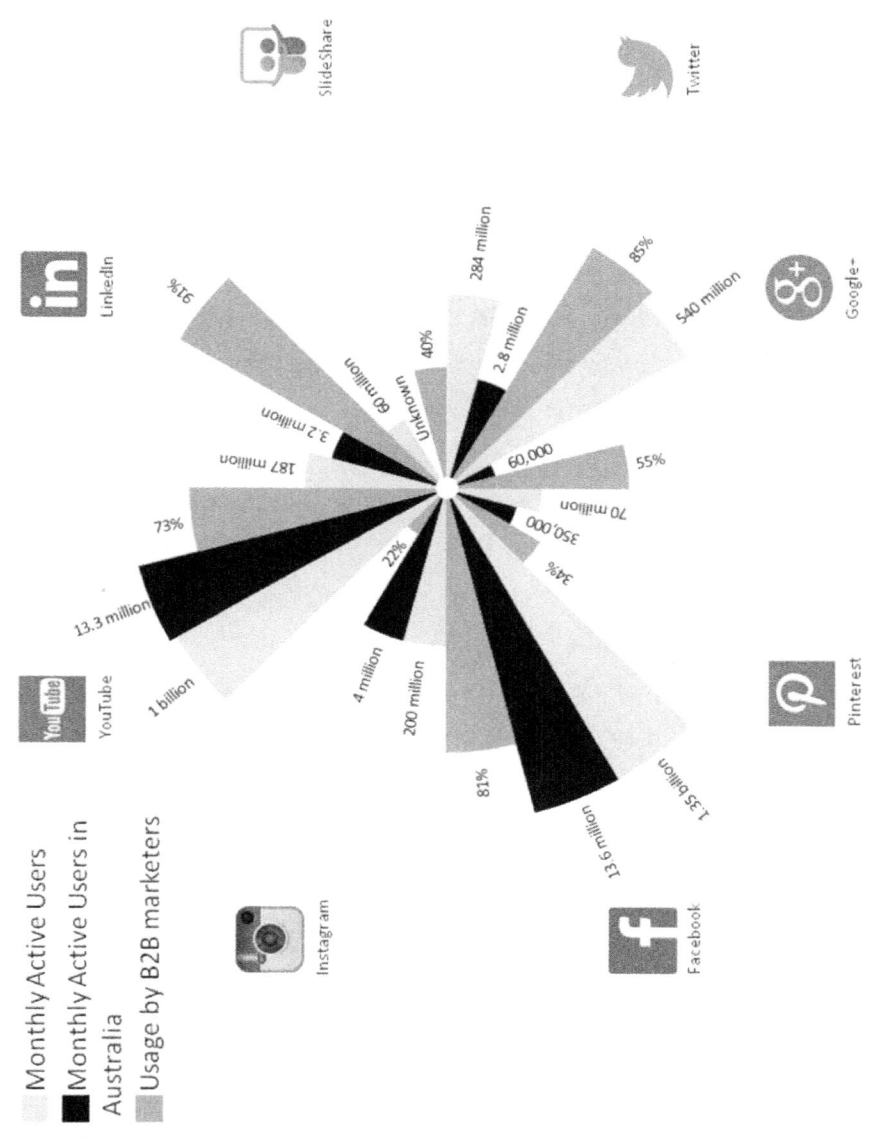

Source: Abramovich, 2014; Narcisse, 2014; Social Dynamite, 2014; Bennett, 2015; Cowling, 2015; Fryrear, 2015. Image: Author.

Exhibit 1.1   The Most Popular Social Media Sites

As I mentioned above, which you can now see, LinkedIn comes out on top, convincing a whopping 91% of B2B marketers to use the site for lead generation. A close second is Twitter with 85%, followed by Facebook with 81% and YouTube with 73%. Google's offering, Google Plus, attracts around half of the B2B marketer population; the possible reasons for this will be discussed later in Chapter 2. Image sharing sites Pinterest and Instagram have not received a significant adoption rate. And SlideShare has yet to see dramatic growth in the B2B marketing space but is predicted to become a major player soon as more and more marketers look to link SlideShare content to its big brother, LinkedIn.

With social media being so prevalent in our lives these days, and in an attempt to omit all but the most beneficial content in this book, I will only briefly describe each of the eight sites in the next chapter to determine if they can help achieve the objectives of a B2B social media strategy. As a result, more time can be dedicated to discussing the best practices and daily tasks for each site that are of main concern to business owners and digital marketers.

If you're interested in learning more about the eight social media sites outlined in this book, as well as some of the other websites and apps available today, then check out some fantastic and often-humorous books including Lon Safko's in-depth introduction to social media in The Social Media Bible (2012) and Gary Vaynerchuk's no holds barred guide to the dos and don'ts of using social media in Jab, Jab, Jab, Right Hook: How to Tell Your Story in a Noisy Social World (2013).

While managing several social media profiles seems like a daunting task, don't make the mistake of thinking consistent social media activity requires bottomless pits of money and teams of internet marketing gurus. This book will show you how to take advantage of social media with the resources you already have available, and the first place to start is with creating objectives.

The Top 4 Objectives: Dynamic, Not Static

Objectives for using social media include enhanced brand awareness, higher search rankings, increased website traffic, cost-effective advertising, and more importantly for B2B companies, lead generation. Lead generation is important here because it validates the return on investment of ongoing social media activities. But while many social media experts advise marketers to focus more on users' attitude of the brand and observe who is sharing brand content on social media, others argue that social signals such as how many users follow the brand and share content provide a more measurable indication of success; especially at first.

Whether you decide to focus on social signals or brand sentiment, you must be prepared to commit to a daily routine of content creation and wait patiently for meaningful results that meet your objectives. Your results, then, should be measured in alignment with your marketing objectives and have a realistic target date for their accomplishment.

You will likely have both long-range and ongoing objectives for using social media. But remember to include short-term goals. Having meaningful short-term goals has the benefit of increasing motivation in the short term in addition to increasing commitment to the goal over the long-term.

Combining the benefits of pursuing both short-term and long-term goals and both quantifiable and unquantifiable results, the following are just four examples of objectives that can provide underlying support to a B2B social media strategy:

- Each social media site allows companies to diversify their communication style while maintaining a consistent tone aligned with brand values.
  Objective 1: Increase social media presence and develop a unique online brand persona.

- Social media profiles help direct new visitors to the official business website or a unique landing page, which can be designed to collect visitor information via enquiry forms.
  Objective 2: Generate two new leads per month

and develop current business connections.

- Word of mouth heavily influences buyer behaviour and social media provides a medium for clients to interact with businesses and forward their reviews to others.

  Objective 3: Engage in two-way interaction with clients, customers and other professionals within similar industries to build brand awareness and develop new business contacts.

- When searching for a business on search engines, a brand's social media profiles are often positioned high in the search results.

  Objective 4: Ensure social profiles appear in search results within three months.

While these are just four possible examples of objectives you can have—and probably represent the most typical for businesses on social media—objectives are never static. Having dynamic objectives means you can add, change, and delete objectives as dictated by your results and available resources.

Anytime objective are changed, however, remember that objectives with timeframes for their achievement and keeping them in view at all times gives your social media specialist or team a boost of motivation and always directing efforts towards those objectives. Clearly stating objectives for a social media campaign also makes it easier to determine which social media platforms will deliver the anticipated outcomes and which ones will not. And social media platform selection is the focus of the next chapter.

CHAPTER ONE ACTION STEPS:

❑ Get your employees and stakeholders together and as a group agree upon your company's objectives for using social media. Don't worry about coming up with overly detailed objectives at this stage since this is likely your first foray into social media and no past results exist which could help predict comprehensive future objectives.

❑ Include as many measurable objectives as possible as these will better determine if your strategy is working.

❑ Write objectives down and stick them up on the wall in clear sight of everyone involved in the success of the strategy.

❑ Go online and read a summary about any of the eight social media sites you're not familiar with before moving on to the next chapter.

CHAPTER TWO:
SOCIAL MEDIA PLATFORM CHOICE

"Build it, and they will come" only works in the movies. Social Media is a "build it, nurture it, engage them and they may come and stay."
- SETH GODIN

CHAPTER CONTENTS

- 2015 Social Media Map
- Popular Social Media Platforms
- Other Social Media Platforms

Overdrive Interactive's Social Media Map

The way to decide which social media platforms to select begins by establishing the amount of currently available resources you have at your disposal and then aligning your business objectives with the advantages of each platform. And while many social media sites exist—and with many more emerging every year (see the Social Media Map and Conversation Prism)—it is not recommended that any business spreads its resources too thinly across many platforms and then struggle to generate consistent engagement on any of them.

The 2015 Social Media Map created by Overdrive Interactive is, as self-described, a snapshot of the evolving social media landscape. Almost every subcategory on the map can present opportunities to assist in a B2B social media strategy from social networks and social recruiting to content discovery and social media tracking and searching. I present the map here to show you how many different kinds of platforms there are to engage with potential clients and why it's not necessary to tackle them all because they all require unique content strategies and most simply won't welcome brands to register for an account—and get accused of spamming.

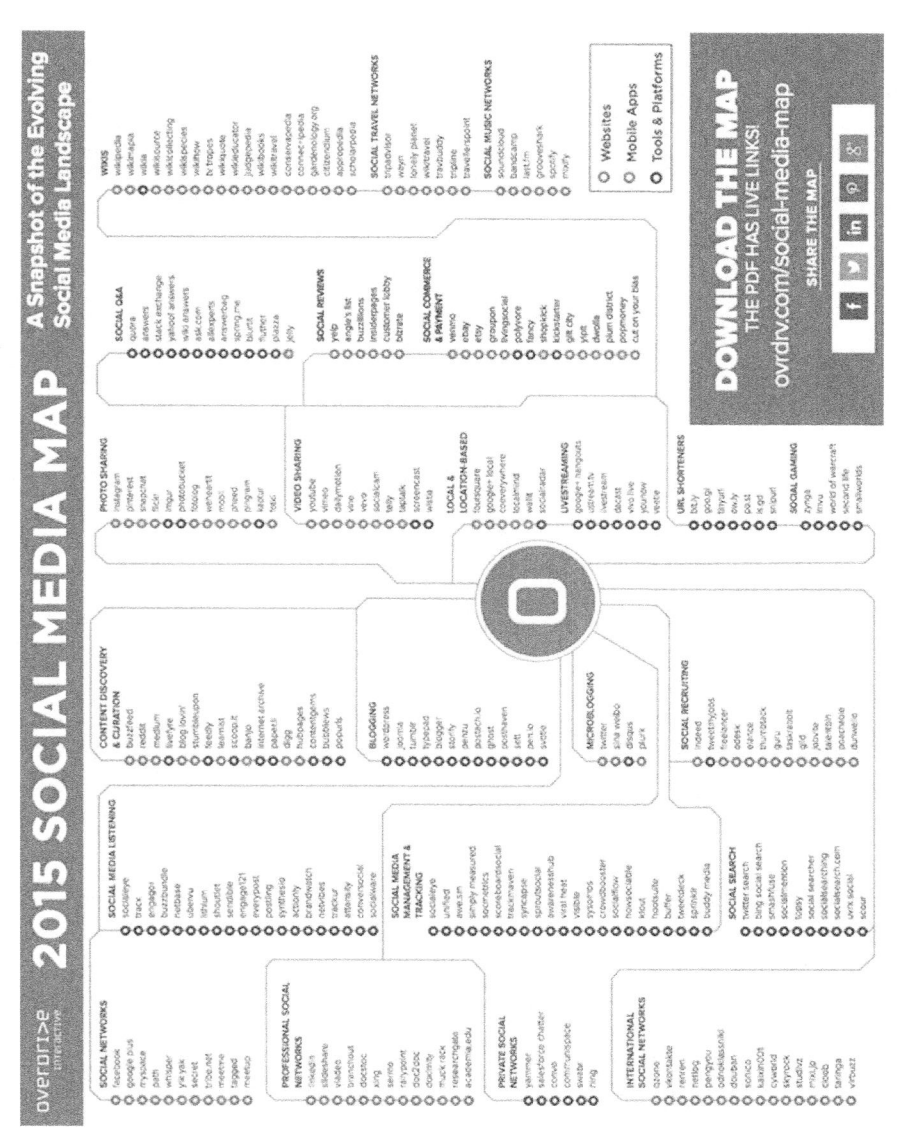

Source: Overdrive Interactive

Exhibit 2.1 The 2015 Social Media Map

We'll follow the lead of B2B marketers and examine the top eight social media platforms for B2B businesses next, and give other possible social media platforms a brief introduction later.

What Are the Top 8 Social Media Platforms for B2B Businesses?
LinkedIn

LinkedIn is best known for being a business-oriented social media platform mainly used by professionals for the purposes of networking in addition to its increasing popularity as a job search and recruitment resource.

LinkedIn offers a quick way for users to connect with other industry professionals for a number of reasons.

- **Market research**
  Saving money and effort by taking advantage of research performed by other companies and shared on LinkedIn profiles.

- **Establishing a company's brand image**
  Posting status updates directly from the source with no alteration from the media adds credibility to the news.

- **Developing relationships with current clients**
  Unlike sites such as Facebook, which cater more to B2C relationships, LinkedIn facilitates better interaction between professional connections.

- **Engaging with new prospects in various target markets**

  As much as a quarter of industrial buyers source industrial products and services directly from LinkedIn.

A 2010 study of LinkedIn found that it was responsible for driving more leads to B2B websites than any other social media site—277% more effective than Twitter and Facebook (Walgrove, 2015)—with almost two thirds of B2B companies having secured at least one new client through the site. Years later, LinkedIn still reportedly outperforms other social media sites, driving over 80% of all B2B social media leads and convincing 63% of B2B marketers to judge LinkedIn as the most effective social media platform for lead generation.

Yet, other studies give props to Twitter, stating that it beats LinkedIn by 9 to 1 in the lead generations stakes. Regardless of which study you believe, it appears that companies on LinkedIn are mainly using the platform for recruitment purposes rather than for marketing, which accounts for the majority of user activity on the site.

SlideShare

SlideShare, purchased in 2012 by LinkedIn, is a website that allows users to upload and share their own presentations and view and download presentations uploaded by other users. It's basically a way to share your

PowerPoint presentations publicly and educate (or entertain) internet users with your knowledge; although you often have to trawl through a lot of useless fluff to find content gold published by major international organisations and government agencies. As a high ranking site, SlideShare presentations with optimised transcription text and outbound links can boost search rankings, with increased visitors to a website being the result of higher rankings.

SlideShare presentations can be embedded on third-party websites also, which all link back to the presentation owner's website and provide a further boost to website traffic. Another of the powerful and measurable ways to generate leads from SlideShare is the ability to capture reader information on the final slide, which can even be collected from websites featuring embedded presentations.

When Forbes described SlideShare as the "quiet giant of content marketing", it highlighted the fact that many B2B marketers are hesitant to adopt the platform as part of their strategy (see Exhibit 1.1). This may be due to an uncertainty over its effectiveness, a reluctance to allocate resources to creating graphical content when posting text updates on other sites can be just as effective, or simply conquering the learning curve of assembling presentations on the site.

Twitter
Twitter is a free microblogging service—frequently

utilised more as a broadcasting platform for brands, celebrities and individuals rather than for two-way social interaction—where users post text messages, better known as tweets. Tweets have a 140-character limit that can include website links and images. Rather than a hindrance, the 140-character limit is actually an effective policy for mobile marketing.

With up to 70% of executives researching products and services on their mobile device before make purchasing decisions, Twitter is one of the most popular mobile-oriented outlets used by executives looking to quickly discover valuable snippets of information. Of course, it is important for B2B marketers to recognise that they have to battle not only with their competitors but also with all other brands who are all shouting in unison for prime position on prospects' Twitter feeds. As a result, as much as 50% of B2B marketers who use the platform are sceptical of its effectiveness.

Twitter was instrumental in advancing the way users search for content through the use of keywords preceded with the # symbol, also known as hashtags. So much so, in fact, that Google has recently partnered with the microblogging site to display tweets in Google search results. This can be incredibly useful to a social media marketer when researching relevant content from recent Twitter conversations via Google. Additionally, Twitter offers a way for B2B companies to announce partnerships and cross promote content to two sets of followers. This can be especially valuable if you are a small B2B company aiming to generate online awareness because you can profit from the greater social media investment and larger fan base of a bigger brand.

Google+

Google+ ("Google Plus") is the social media arm of the world's most popular search engine. In contrast to individual platforms such as LinkedIn and Twitter, Google+ has the advantage of being integrated with all other Google services including Chrome, Maps, Gmail, Calendar, YouTube, Shopping, Play, Docs, AdWords, and Analytics, making it easy for marketing professionals to manage many facets of the business from a single account. Moreover, because the mobile operating system Android is developed by Google, B2B marketers can provide smartphone and tablet users with a rich Google+ experience.

There can be no uncertainty of the greatest benefit of having a business Google+ profile: Search. Google executes the vast majority, approximately 70%, of all internet searches and is the number one resource for B2B buyers investigating products and services. Additionally, since over two-thirds of people will not explore search results beyond the first page and generally find what they are looking for within the top five results on that first page, it's vital you do what you can to get your website closer to that first-page, top-five position.

Google, in short, dominates the search market, heavily influences many decision makers, and presents the most relevant links within the top five results. This means B2B marketers must do what they can to feature in the top half of the first page for keywords relevant to their business activities. One potential way to boost search rankings is to create a Google+ profile because Google will assign a greater weight to its own social media outlet than others. Beyond merely creating an account, however, Google will rely on social signals, such as when other users view and share your content, to govern the position of company websites in the search results.

B2B marketers must be aware that as Google algorithms become more and more sophisticated, search results will become even more personalised to each user based on past search requests, social media behaviour, location, purchase history, and other factors. This means that B2B marketers should not rely completely on search rankings when performing analysis of their keywords, and at the same time not get discouraged when the brand does not appear to have higher rankings despite consistent and increasing activity on Google+ (or any social media platform).

Another thing to be aware of is the predicted death of Google+ by social media commentators. Sure, the shocking number of empty Google+ profiles make it feel like a ghost town—sadly, brands expect a harvest by simply planting seeds and neglecting to water them—but many businesses have a fine reputation among Google+ communities. I believe the argument over the future of Google+ stems from it's phenomenal initial growth and subsequent failure to claim the throne of social media king from Facebook. To be fair, every new social media platform is proclaimed to be the next Facebook but never comes close to living up to its hype. The point is that Google+ can improve brand awareness online but only if you follow the golden rule of social media: consistency.

Pinterest

Pinterest is a photo-sharing website mainly used for visual bookmarking; using images as links that direct users to an external website. Pinterest offers B2B marketers an extra channel to disseminate content and drive more traffic to the company website or landing page by 'pinning' images to image boards on their profile. Company updates, past campaigns, and recent research results can all be repurposed into images, saving B2B marketers and graphic designers the extra workload required to create brand new content exclusively for Pinterest. Images can include a short description and hashtags, but in contrast to the very short lifespan of tweets, images pinned on Pinterest remain searchable on Google for much longer.

There is a downside to using Pinterest that both Pinterest users and B2B marketers should be aware of.

Many fake profiles exist and scammers are rampant in their efforts to post images for the purposes of directing users to spam or scam websites. Pinterest administrators do claim that they try their best to prevent this and will block profiles and links considered or reported to be spam, including when users try to protect their anonymity on Pinterest through third-party software.

Another useful point to note about Pinterest is its user demographics. With the most popular categories listed as women's apparel, travel, food, crafts, DIY, and home decor, it may come as no surprise that in certain countries (the UK is an anomaly in this case) about three quarters of Pinterest users are women.

Facebook

Facebook is the world's most popular social media site, with about 20% of the entire population managing an account. With a proposed push towards mobile users in the coming years, Facebook stands poised to further increase their user base and revenues. Such an increase in revenue allows digital companies such as Facebook to develop new technologies, which have the potential to reduce advertising costs for marketers.

As your Facebook business page gains followers, more can be learned about your followers' interests, which allows you to produce better targeted content. And Facebook rewards businesses that are performing well in terms of ratings and user engagement by showing more of their posts in followers' news feeds. But don't get too carried away with follower acquisition because as the number of Facebook followers goes beyond a certain amount, the diverse range of user interests makes it difficult to find commonalities among users and post engagement suffers as a result.

In view of the fact that almost every person in the world with access to an Internet connection has a Facebook account, it can be difficult, even for B2C marketers, to spread marketing material. The only way to target specific demographics in Facebook is to use paid advertising, which has been found to generate disappointing results compared with displaying ads on other websites. Users simply do not want to be spammed with unsolicited advertisements taking up space on their news feed.

The only issue I have with Facebook for small B2B companies is that because most users are not included in your target audience, it makes less sense to mass spread information on Facebook rather than LinkedIn when resources may dictate that only one of those platforms can be adopted.

Instagram

Instagram, owned by and fully integrated with Facebook, is a photo and video-sharing mobile application. Instagram differs from its competitor, Pinterest, by offering a space for people to share photos taken by their smartphones while 'in the moment' and use hashtags to describe image content in addition to where the photo was taken and the emotions felt at the time. For marketers, Instagram is a free venue for spreading content to millions of mobile users with a fondness for images. And reach is further increased when users promote Instagram content on their Facebook profiles.

Apart from the limitations of being a mobile-only platform, the weaknesses of Instagram from a B2B perspective, apart from the condemnation of overtly branded posts, are that:

1. Like tweets, posts to Instagram have a very short existence before being crushed into obscurity under the weight of new posts.

2. Compared to Pinterest, images do not have the capacity to be shared directly from the app or include backlinks to websites.

3. Instagram users are generally younger people with a more diverse range of interests.

YouTube

Responsible for some of the most memorable viral hits in history, YouTube is the largest video-sharing website on the internet. So large, in fact, that in 2014 it was estimated that YouTube servers store more than 300 hours of new footage every minute.

The impressive array of sharing options, including the ability to embed videos on third-party websites, Facebook, Google+, and many other websites, mean businesses profit from the extended reach of marketing content.

The major downside of including YouTube in a content marketing strategy is the time required to plan, produce and publish videos in addition to generating eye-catching titles and optimised description text. The argument that even an impromptu video shot on a smartphone has the potential to reach a million views may not hold up in a marketing sense where businesses aim to pass on the brand message as the video spreads. Just to be clear, I like YouTube for content marketing and lead generation. What I don't like to do is advocate YouTube for time-poor B2B businesses.

The Conversation Prism with YOU in the Middle – Other Social Media Platforms

You can see from The Conversation Prism in Exhibit 2.2 and the 2015 Social Media Map from earlier that connections between businesses, between customers, and between businesses and customers are happening in an incredible number of digital public spheres. Many brands are having great success with podcasting, blogging, answer, and social bookmarking sites, for example.

Can you get involved in them all? Sure you can. But it

would take one hell of an effort and the return on investment probably wouldn't make it worthwhile.

Exhibit 2.2   The Conversation Prism

It is much better—and less stressful—to focus your efforts on a select few platforms where most of your target audience congregate. That's not to say you can't become an expert in the Reddit community or regularly respond to user comments on Yahoo Answers at some point in the future. In fact, I'd recommend looking into some of the other niche sites in the future once you've got a handle on your selected platforms from the top eight as long as it doesn't steal resources from all the hard work you've put in to building a strong following on other platforms.

CHAPTER TWO ACTION STEPS:

❑ Make a brief list of the advantages and disadvantages of using each of the top eight platforms and how each will help or hinder achieving your objectives.

❑ Go through your list and decide on four social media platforms that you will use in your social media strategy based on your currently available resources.

❑ If you don't have one already, register for an account on each of your chosen platforms using a pseudo-personal account and familiarise yourself with the layout, features and typical user behaviour.

❑ Follow some of your competitors and B2B companies in other regions that offer similar services to yours to see how they are using the platform.

Chapter 3 will discuss the best practices for consistent branding, including setting up branded user profile names. I suggest waiting until you have read the next chapter before registering your branded accounts.

CHAPTER THREE:
BEST PRACTICE GUIDE

Do it badly; do it slowly; do it fearfully; do it any way you have to, but do it.
- STEVE CHANDLER

CHAPTER CONTENTS

- Best Practice Guide for Each Platform
- Target Audience Interests
- Time Zones
- Rule of Thirds

Do it Right, Do it Fearfully – Best Practice Guide For Each Platform

I use the term 'Best Practice Guide' with a condition. While it certainly offers many tips on making the most of available features within each of the eight most popular social media platforms, it does not cover what not to do on each platform. I want to first open your eyes to what's possible on each platform so you can make an informed decision to the right ones for you. Similarly, I want you to create a policy for social media use—content style, tone of voice, responding to comments, etc.—that's unique to your brand. I'll cover these topics in Chapters 4 and 7 but for now let's look at succeeding on social media.

Best Practice Guide for LinkedIn

- **Showcase Pages**

One of the ways to build a larger, more targeted following on LinkedIn is via Showcase Pages; dedicated business pages primarily used to highlight initiatives of various business units within an organisation. This allows LinkedIn users to follow only those sections of a business with which they have a specific interest in. IBM is a great example of a business making excellent use of showcase pages on LinkedIn. Exhibits 3.1 and 3.2 show how IBM have created their Showcase Pages—with unique profile images and tens of thousands of followers for each page—and how their most popular page is set up.

Exhibit 3.1   IBM Showcase Page List

LinkedIn allows you to create up to ten unique showcase pages for every parent company page. Think of these extra pages not as additional work but as a space to highlight each of your business units or services. You don't have to publish to all of them every time you are scheduled to post content on LinkedIn. In fact, it's better practice to post an assortment of content to your individual showcase pages and on a rotating basis, and let other LinkedInners know about your new posts through regular updates on your main company page.

Exhibit 3.2   IBM Cloud Showcase Page

Perform a quick search of your local and national

competitors to discover whether or not they are taking advantage of showcase pages. If not, then this presents an excellent opportunity for you to dominate this space in your industry.

To create a showcase page, go to your company page and click the 'Create a Showcase Page' option from the top-right dropdown menu.

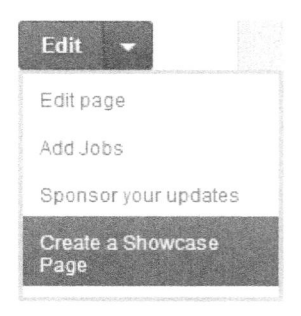

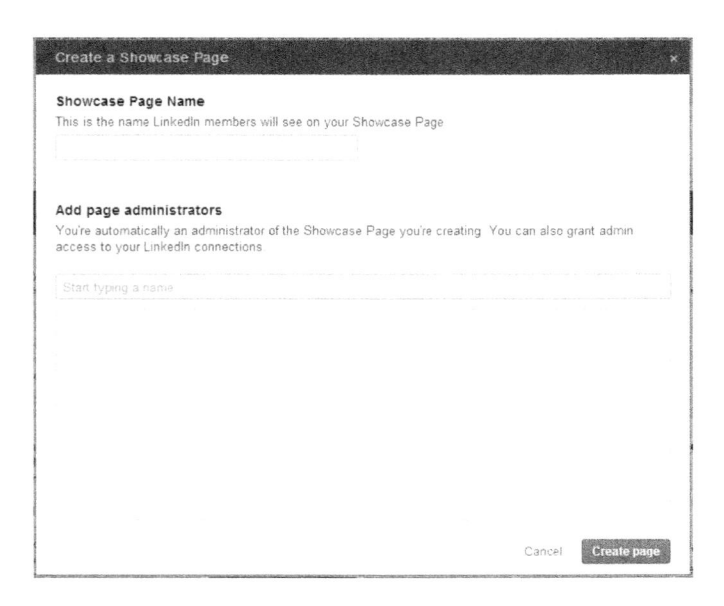

Exhibit 3.3 (a)(b) How to Create a Showcase Page

- **LinkedIn Pulse**

LinkedIn Pulse is where you'll find trending content and popular articles centred around what you are interested in and who you follow. It is a quick way to discover influencers in your industry that you can follow. But research should be your secondary goal. Because many other LinkedInners will be consuming new articles from this section, getting your own content sitting side by side with these popular articles is your main goal.

Exhibit 3.4 is how the main page of Pulse looks (on the day I took the screenshot, of course). You'll notice that it lists five popular articles on the left, with the topmost article open on the right. Well, it actually works on an infinite scroll, i.e. if you scroll through the first article, it will continue to populate the page with new articles well after you finish reading the top five. This means this morning's articles will have a short lifespan before being knocked down the pecking order by the evening's or the next day's articles.

To overcome this issue, always give your content a longer existence by sharing them on your company page and sharing on your company blog (if you have one).

To post a new article on LinkedIn Pulse, simply go to the main Pulse page and click the button 'Publish a post', and add your image, headline, text, and tags.

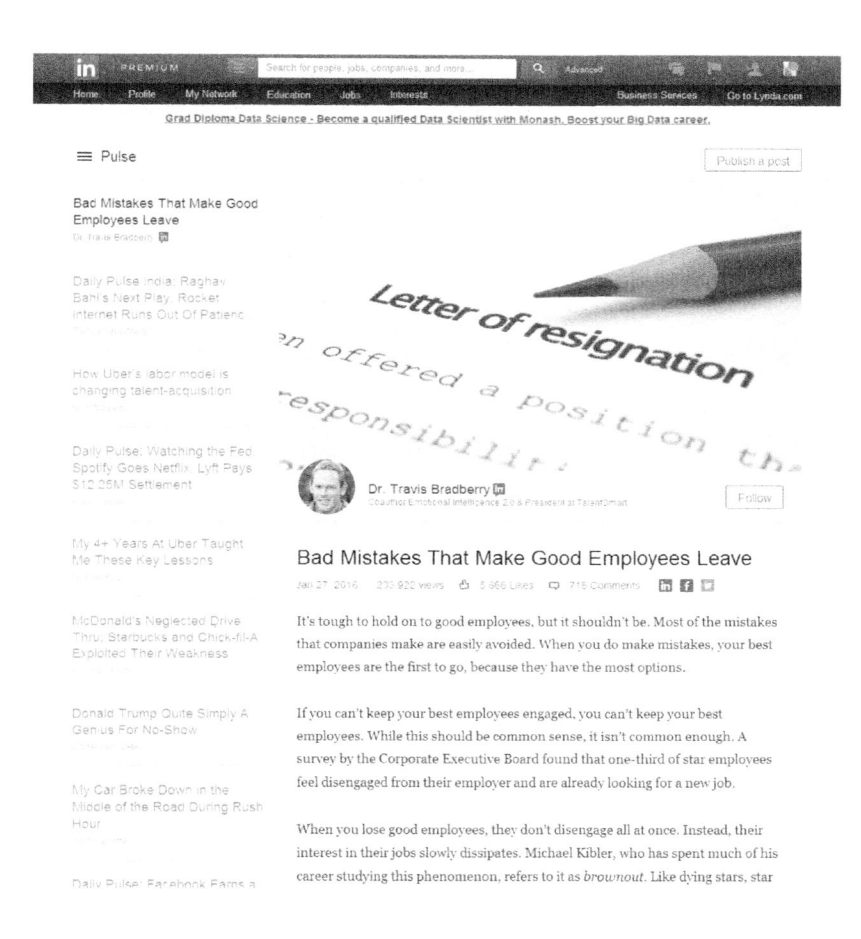

Exhibit 3.4   LinkedIn Pulse

Best Practice Guide for SlideShare

- ### Slide Design

SlideShare is nice and simple. It's basically about publishing original, share-worthy presentations. The basic principles of creating such presentations, then, include a skilled use of colours, fonts, and images. SlideShare presentations are around 14 slides on average and contain roughly 25 words per slide. That gives you 14 opportunities to blow your audience away with great design and use just 350 words to educate or influence your audience to engage with you. But eye-catching design and persuasive content should not take away from the golden rule: keep it clear and simple.

The best way to follow the golden rule is through consistency; consistent fonts, consistent colour palette, consistent message, and images that consistently align with your message. And remember to include your brand's logo and a clickable call to action (after the third slide). Ethos3 re a brand making fantastic presentations as you can see from an example in Exhibit 3.5.

Exhibit 3.5   Ethos3 SlideShare Presentation Design

- **Description Text**
Your description text is how people will find your

presentation from searching online—apart from clicking through from your posts on your other social media profiles. That means you'll want to ensure it's very easy to be found.

One of the clever things SlideShare does is to automatically pull text from your presentation and populate the description field. You can capitalise on this by entering keyword-rich text behind the images in your slides so that your slides look great and your transcription text is optimised for Google, Yahoo, and Bing. But this doubles your effort and it's not really necessary. Instead, fill out the description field fully and add a call to action at the end.

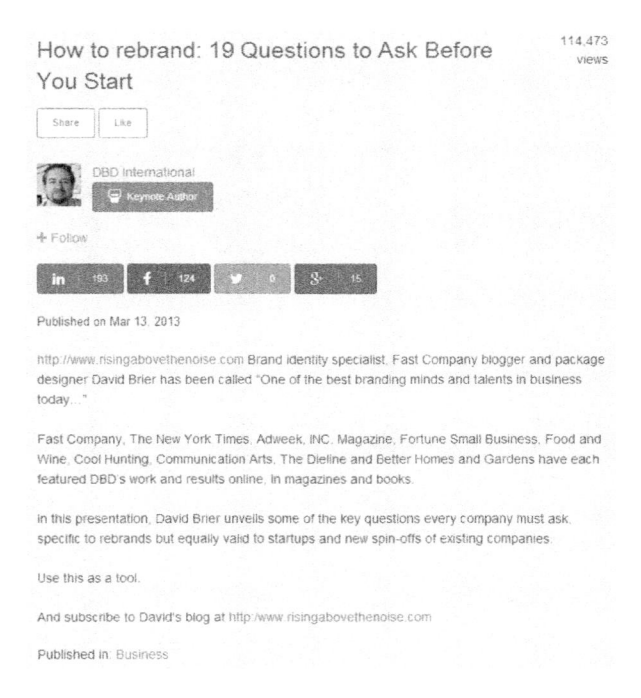

Exhibit 3.6   Example SlideShare Description Text

- **Lead Generation**

Lead generation is made possible on SlideShare by adding lead forms to your presentation. SlideShare walks you through this process and help you capture information from potential clients. Click on the 'Collect Leads' button at the top right after logging in and follow the steps as laid out on the platform.

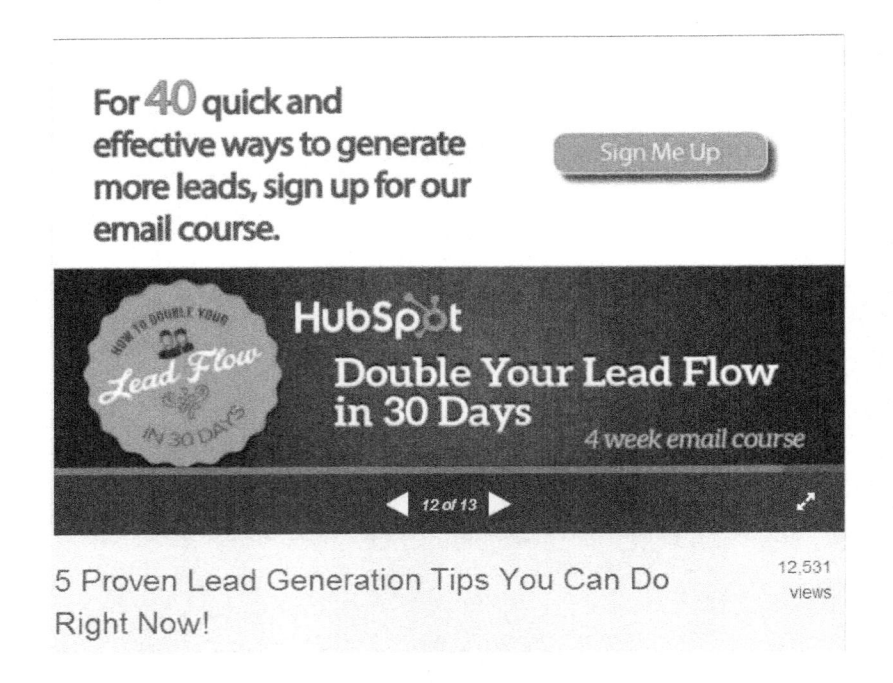

Exhibit 3.7   Example SlideShare Lead Generation Form

Best Practice Guide for Facebook

- **Milestones**

Milestones are like telling a visual story or timeline of the business. Milestones are normally major current and past business-related events that add more visibility to your

Facebook updates. And since milestones work best with engaging images, you can reuse cool vintage photos.

Here's an example of a business page making great use of milestones, AccorHotels Group, although I think they could have more impact in the example shown in Exhibit 3.8 by adding a call to action and link, e.g. "Say bonjour to l'Hotel de la France at www.accorhotels....":

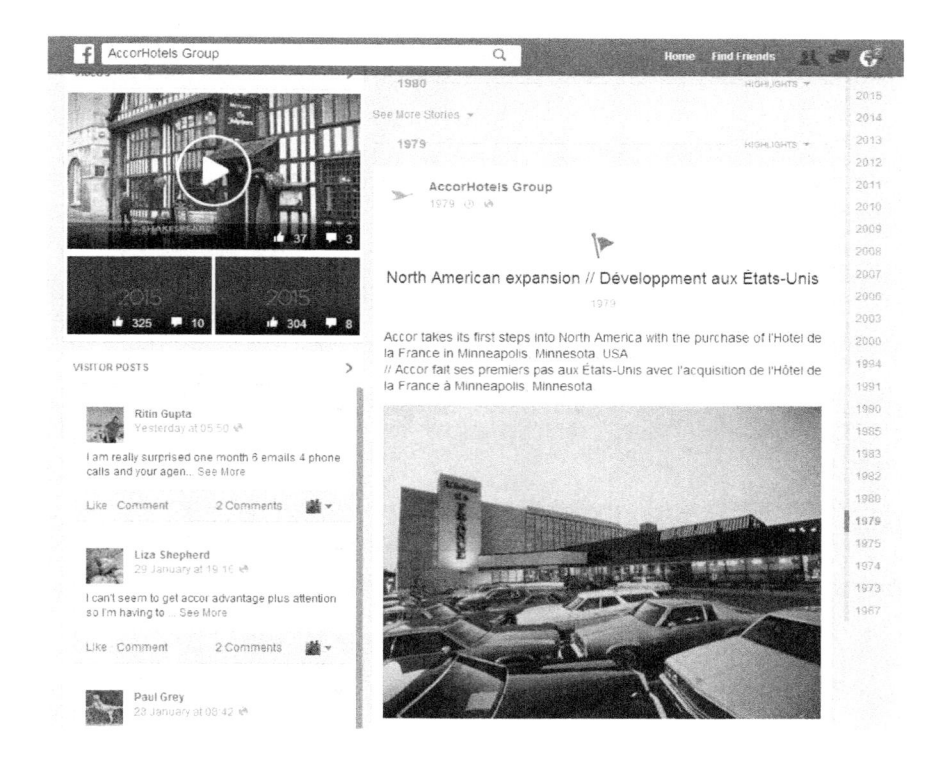

Exhibit 3.8   AccorHotels Group Milestone Example

To create a new milestone, select "Event, Milestone +" and then "Milestone".

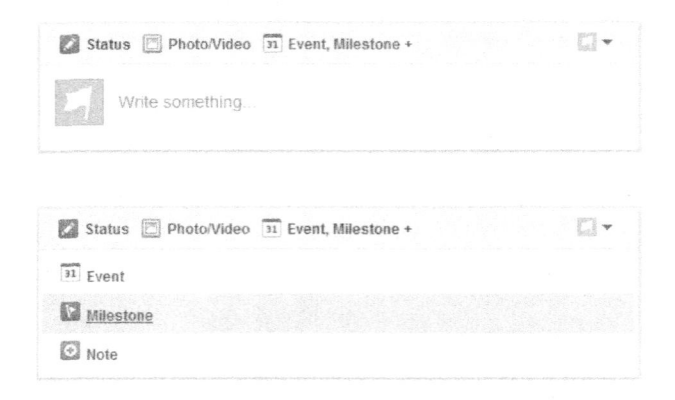

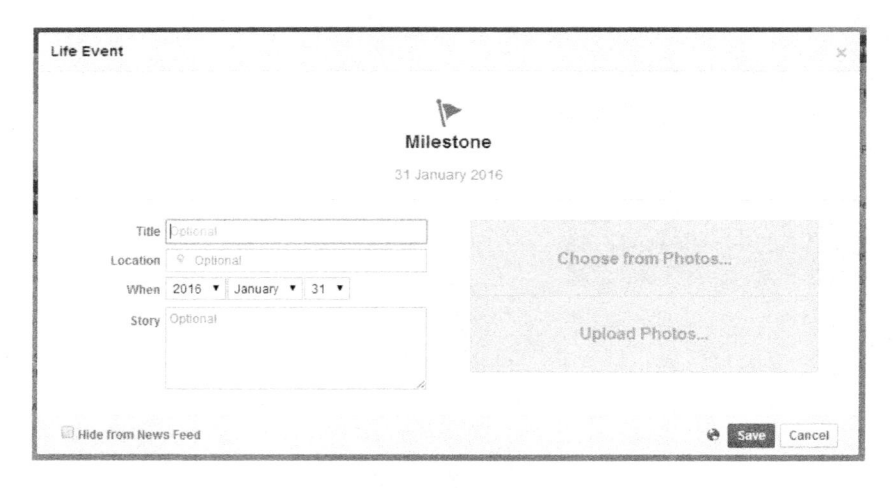

Exhibit 3.9 (a)(b)(c) Creating Milestones on Facebook

Milestones would fall under the branded content type (see Chapter 4 for more details on content types) and only one milestone should be posted at one time.

- **Apps**

Facebook offers many great interactive apps that allow fans to engage with your brand—including make enquiries and sign up for newsletters—straight from Facebook. Here is a perfect example that is integrated on the Salesforce company page:

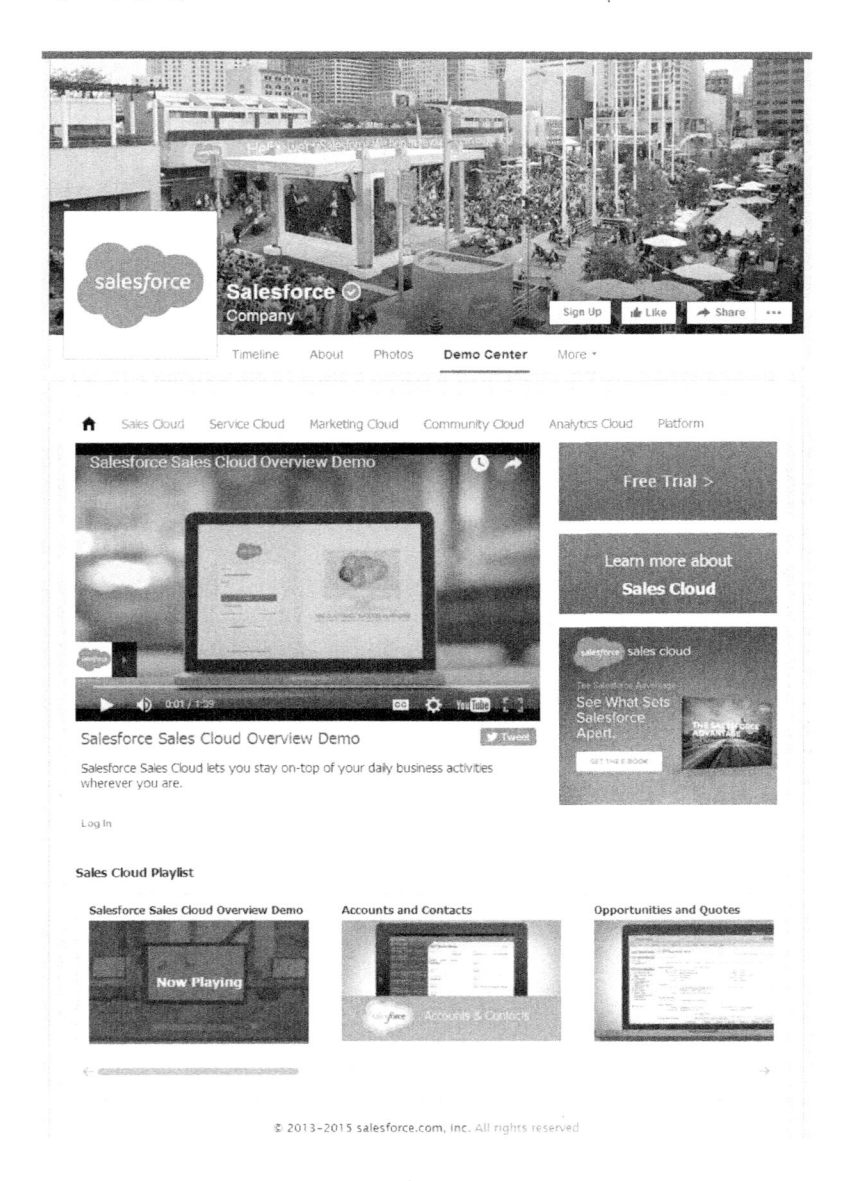

Exhibit 3.10 Salesforce Interactive App

Best Practice Guide for Twitter

- **Tweeting**

Tweets have a very short shelf life, even when using hashtags. This means that it's necessary to say the same thing more than once. Typically, you will tweet the same thing three times in one day, with slightly altered text each time. Considering your current resources, however, you may wish to tweet just twice a day.

In amongst your two branded tweets will be relevant customer tweets and trending influencer retweets, making an average total of at least 4-6 tweets a day. Sharing other's content is a major factor in the success of any social media strategy. Your social media management tool should give you easy access to shareable content from all profiles you currently follow. Others' tweets can then be retweeted immediately or edited and scheduled for later (see Chapter 11 for more details on how to retweet).

- **Hashtags**

Twitter researchers revealed that single-word hashtags with six characters or less perform best. Generally, the best hashtags are the most obvious ones. For your company, this can include hashtags related to your industry, particularly those that are currently trending. Plus, it is good practice to limit the number of hashtags in a single tweet to one or two.

Similarly for branded hashtags, it is best to use two or

three consistently to increase reach for those hashtags. Rather than list hashtags at the end of the text, which uses up valuable character space and reduces interaction, single words or acronyms within the tweet can be transformed into hashtags, while branded hashtags can go at the end before the link.

Here's an example with 111 characters (should be less), a single-word hashtag within the text (using the most obvious and industry-related word for a hashtag), a shortened link, and an interesting graphical image on an iPad:

Exhibit 3.11 HubSpot Example Tweet

- **Character Length**

Tweets should be kept below 100 characters, including links and images, with the optimal length around 65-70 characters. Tweets longer than 100 characters are unlikely to be retweeted because anything the retweeter adds, even just "RT", could take it over the 140 character limit.

Best Practice Guide for Google+

- **Formatting**

Google+ combines features of Facebook and Twitter, making it more like a mini blog site; perfect for linking to instructional posts. This means the ideal post layout should have a title first (less than 60 characters), then a line break, and then a summary of the linked article with either integrated hashtags or hashtags at the end. You can also mention other Google+ users by adding '+' in front of their username.

When scheduling posts in your social media management tool, add a url to the text and it will automatically show up below the post with a clickable thumbnail. Then you can either keep the url as a second clickable link or remove it for a cleaner post.

You can add a little variety to posts by using simple formatting. Here is the list of formatting options:

Bold	=	**Bold**
Italics	=	*Italics*
-Strikethrough-	=	~~Strikethrough~~

The following is an example to highlight all the best practices of Google+ posts above. First line length is 60 characters and has bolded text to become a title. Then there is a few sentences to summarise the linked article and the url, and finally two relevant hashtags.

Exhibit 3.12   Dell Example Google+ Post

Best Practice Guide for Pinterest

• Images

Make the most of real estate on Pinterest's image feed by pinning visually stunning vertical images. Because of Pinterest's column-style layout, images in landscape mode appear much smaller than those in portrait mode. Make sure your images stand out by maximising the height and minimising the width of images you pin to Pinterest.

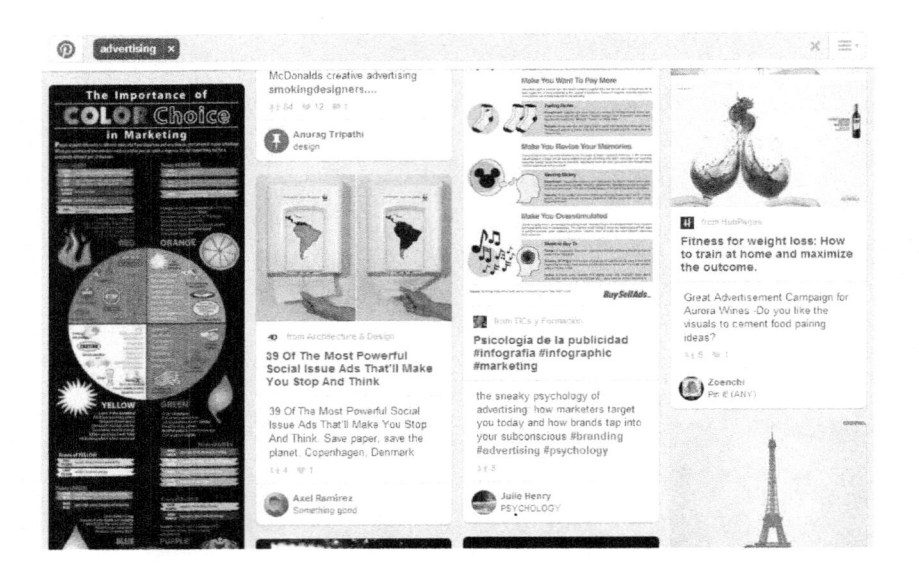

Exhibit 3.13   Vertical Pin Example

• Boards

Like showcase pages on LinkedIn, boards on Pinterest give you an extra avenue to engage with fans who are interested in specific sections of your business. But that's not all you should use them for. You ought to create and maintain other boards that inspire, educate, and entertain.

To achieve this, simply pin images you find while browsing online, while scrolling through other Pinner's boards, and while creating content for your own campaigns such as SlideShare presentations and infographics.

Make sure to keep your boards clean and organised—see Exhibit 3.14 for a fine example of board layout for a B2B brand. Your goal should be to title each board using appropriate keywords and only pin related images to each board. This allows followers to subscribe to the boards that interest them the most and don't get annoyed if irrelevant images appear on their subscribed boards.

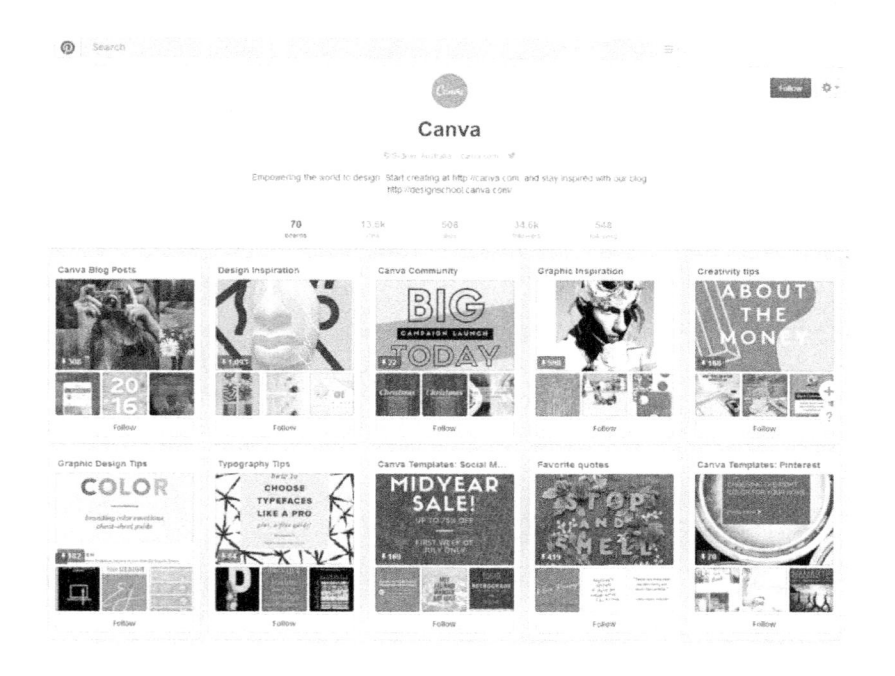

Exhibit 3.14   Canva Pinterest Boards

Best Practice Guide for Instagram

- **Hashtags**

Instagram is a hashtag-fest. And the more hashtags you use the better. In fact, posts with 11 hashtags well outperform posts with less. In addition to your unique branded hashtags, it is good practice to add industry-related and trending hashtags to the end of your Instagram posts.

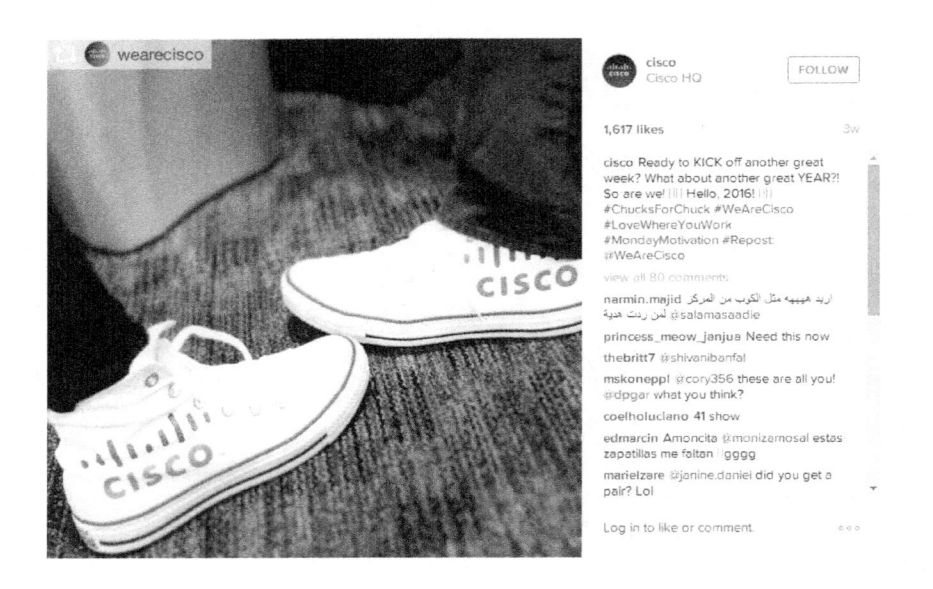

Exhibit 3.15 Hashtags

- **Images**

Hootsuite doesn't support image optimisation for Instagram so you have to crop them before being uploaded and scheduled. The optimal Instagram image size is 1080px by 1080px, which prevents images looking blurry or having jaggy edges when viewed on high-resolution displays.

- **Videos**

15-second videos and gifs are becoming more and more popular on Instagram. At the time of writing, no social media management tool (that I'm aware of) supports uploading and scheduling of videos on Instagram, which means this won't be part of your initial strategy but is worthwhile including in your list of ideas for the future.

Best Practice Guide for YouTube

- **Uploading videos**

If you've never uploaded a video to YouTube before, don't fret. It couldn't be easier. What you need to focus on is how you'll title and describe your video so that it can be found on YouTube and elsewhere online.

I've found that it's best practice to begin your title with your brand name followed by just a few keywords describing the video content. In the description field, feel free to add engaging sentences bullet lists, links to your social profiles, and remember to add a hyperlink for viewers to find more information. See Exhibit 3.16 for an example of this format.

But I urge you to test using various title and description formats to see what works for you.

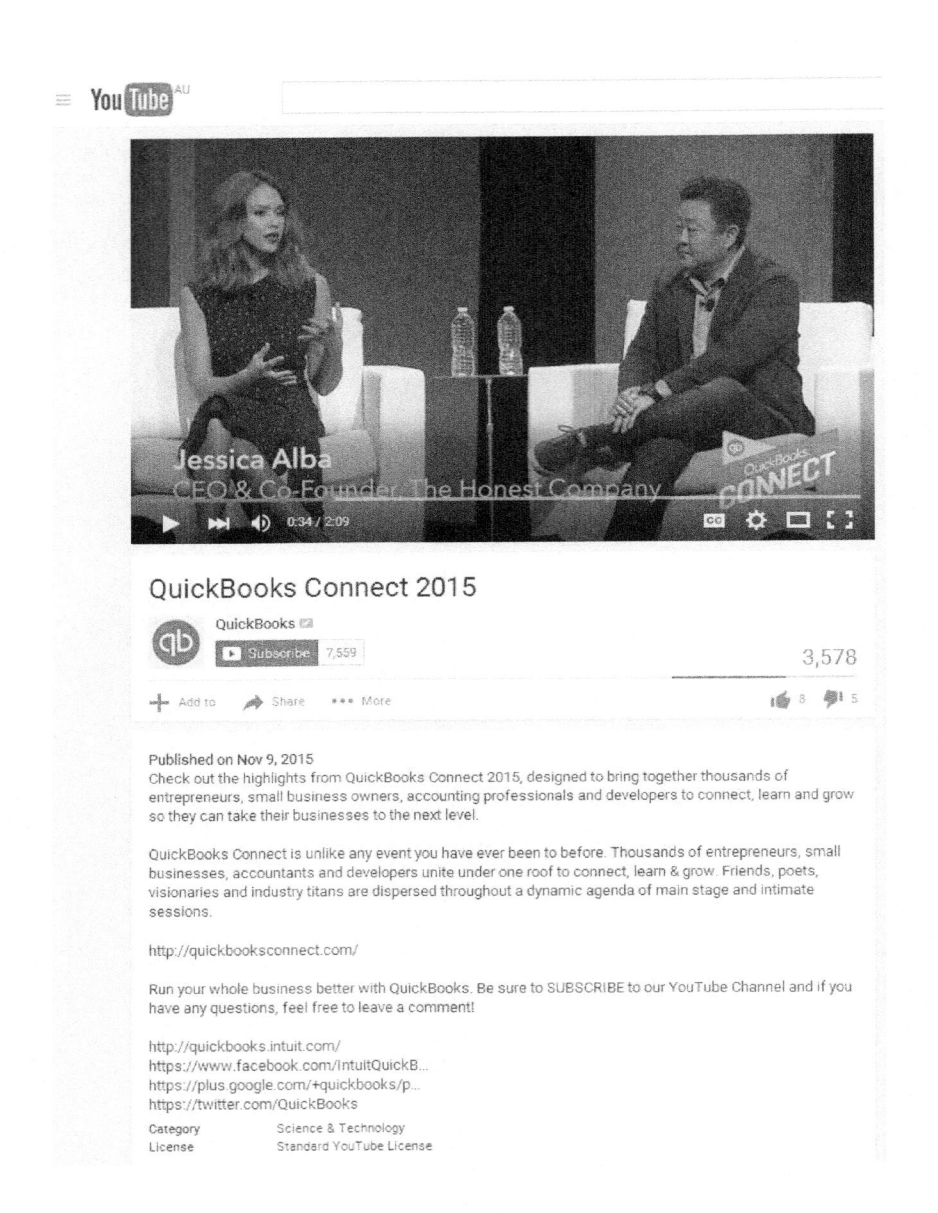

Exhibit 3.16   QuickBooks YouTube Title & Description

- **Video Length**

Social Bakers suggest that YouTube videos between 31 seconds and one minute long generate the most views based on their research into the 300 most-viewed brand channels on YouTube.

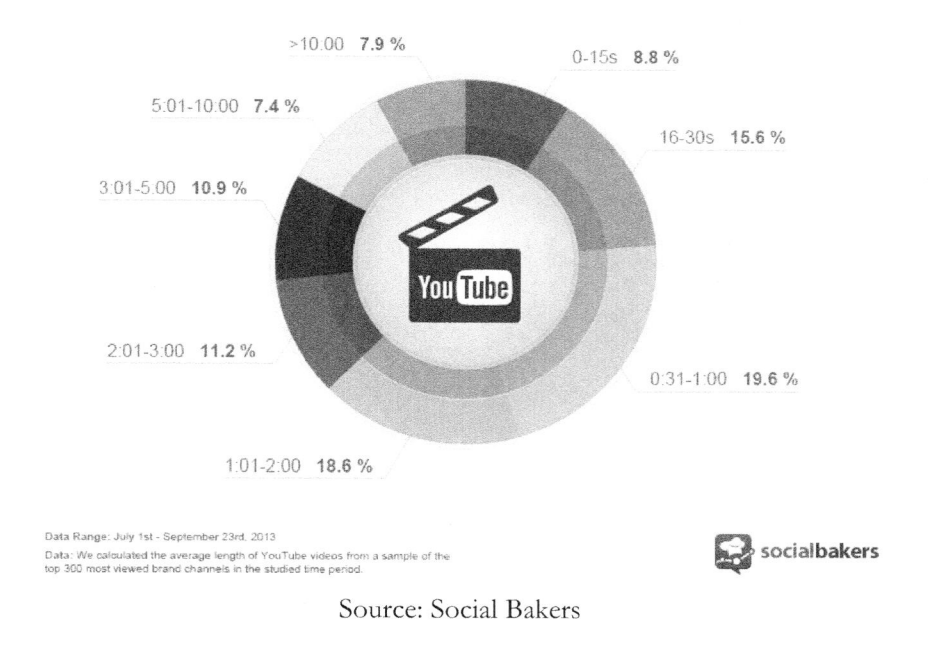

Videos Under Two Minutes Generate the Most YouTube Views

>10.00 **7.9 %**

0-15s **8.8 %**

5:01-10:00 **7.4 %**

16-30s **15.6 %**

3:01-5:00 **10.9 %**

2:01-3:00 **11.2 %**

0:31-1:00 **19.6 %**

1:01-2:00 **18.6 %**

Data Range: July 1st - September 23rd, 2013
Data: We calculated the average length of YouTube videos from a sample of the top 300 most viewed brand channels in the studied time period.

socialbakers

Source: Social Bakers

Exhibit 3.17 YouTube Views by Video Length

Also shown in Exhibit 3.17 is that videos between 16 seconds and two minutes draw the highest percentage of YouTube views. Therefore, you should aim to publish your videos within this brief duration. Fortunately, this means you don't have to stress about keeping your audience engaged for long periods of time. Instead, produce snippets of powerful content and try to influence viewers to get in touch with you.

Social Media Profiles

The first step after selecting which social media platforms you will use is to decide on the username convention for your brand. Having a consistent username ensures fans can easily identify you on each platform. Perform a quick search on each platform to see if your chosen name is available and snatch it before someone else does. If you can't get the name you want, try to modify it slightly while keeping it on-brand and avoiding dashes, underscores or changing an s to a z.

The next step is to update the company profile section across all accounts using branded text and images in addition to embedding website links.

Lisa Gulasy of kunocreative.com outlines seven steps to completing a professional business Twitter profile, which I believe are applicable across all chosen social media profiles. They are:

1. Be brief. For instance, Twitter provides space for 160 characters but using less is better;
2. Outline what you will publish. Clearly state what followers can expect to see in their feeds;
3. Say what you want to be known for;
4. Be original. Write original copy for the company website and each social media channel;
5. Inject personality;
6. Include a call to action; and
7. Use clear language to describe services offered.

I don't believe all seven are necessary for your brand's profile, however. Based on these recommendations, I believe your profiles should have brief yet informative bio text and a link to your website link.

Leaving Your Audience Satisfied – Target Audience Interests

The Uses and Gratifications Theory (UGT) suggests that people actively seek out media to satisfy five needs:

1. The need to find information.
2. The need to see what people are up to in the news.
3. The need to be entertained.
4. The need to be part of society.
5. The need to escape their stressful life for an hour or two.

All users have their own specific goals for accessing social media sites—whether it's for information seeking, reading the latest news, being entertained, getting involved in conversations, or just watching funny videos. This means interests across gender, ages, locations, and platforms can vary widely and make it challenging to share content that will engage everyone. Knowing how to pinpoint the interests of your target audience is key.

There are some basic ways to discover who your audience is and what kind of content they engage with. As a B2B company, you can instantly narrow your target audience since you will likely want to target professionals within your industry or a variety of related industries.

With this is mind, the first step is identifying the job titles of the people you mainly deal with as well as the stakeholders those people communicate with before making business decisions. That means you could be targeting business owners, CEOs, marketing managers, sales executives, and other business professionals.

Where these types of people are likely to hang out online is unknown—everywhere, I'll bet. But since these people will digest information, read news, be entertained, and join communities on LinkedIn, Twitter, Facebook, YouTube, Google+, SlideShare, Pinterest, and Instagram, you'll find out what these people like by doing some covert research on these platforms.

On LinkedIn, for instance, you may read an interesting article revealing the usefulness of a new business app and notice that several of the commentators represent businesses with the potential to seek your services. Now you know your target audience enjoys reading about new technology. Continue with your investigation in a similar manner on other platforms.

If you have an email list already, you can supplement your research by asking your subscribers straight out what their challenges are and what information they seek to resolve these problems. This will be a more time-consuming operation and the results will be skewed towards only those individuals who responded to your survey but you will end up with solid data to support your content strategy. Just as you would an email list, the data collected will be more valuable if you can divide the target audience in your region into segments.

So if you managed a travel company, for example, you may decide to divide the target audience in your region into segments by age and gender, and, based on your research, note the interests for each segment as follows:

- **Male Audience (18-44)**
  To hear about offers, promotions and competitions, stay up to date with exclusive brand news, learn about cool new gadgets and technology, watch sports, and be entertained.

- **Female Audience (18-44)**
  To be inspired with travel ideas, learn new tips, engage in conversations, stay fit and healthy, get good deals on fashion items, and hear about offers, promotions and competitions.

- **Male & Female Audience (45-65)**
  To be entertained, stay up to date with news and current events, discover group travel opportunities, learn new recipes, and network with friends, family, and community groups.

Your social media profiles must then align with the target audience's interests and follow the rule of thirds (I'll explain this rule in a moment) by posting industry news, promoting new resorts, publicising travel-related events and festivals, suggesting outdoor activities and cool things to do, asking questions, announcing offers, promotions and competitions, providing travel tips and ideas, and sharing funny images, videos and jokes.

Content overkill, right?

To simplify things, make a list of the five key content types that are gratifying for all audience segments. You can always reassess this at regular intervals.

Cross-referencing the fan interests of each audience segment as shown in the table in Exhibit 3.18 on the following page suggests that the main content types to target should fall under these five general categories: Industry and Your Brand, Offers, Travel, Tips & Tricks, and Entertainment.

	Male Audience (18–44)	Female Audience (18–44)	Males & Females (45–65)
Platforms	LinkedIn, Google+, Facebook, Twitter	LinkedIn, Pinterest, Facebook, Instagram	Facebook, Instagram, YouTube
Interests	Offers, Promotions & Competitions	Travel Ideas & Tips	Group Travel
	Exclusive Brand News	Offers, Promotions & Competitions	News & Current Events
	Video Games & Cool Toys/Inventions	Entertainment, TV Shows & Reality TV	Connect with Family & Friends
	Lad Websites & Social Profiles	Fitness, Health & Beauty	Holiday & Travel Videos
	Sports Products, Stars & Teams	Fashion & Beauty/Cosmetics	Food & Recipe Ideas

Exhibit 3.18   Fan Interests by Gender/Age

Serving Clients Across Continents and Time Zones

It is entirely possible that you have potential clients located in different time zones; serving clients across continents or even nationwide. Local-focussed businesses can skip this section and return to it in the future if you expand nationally or internationally. I'll illustrate this challenge with a situation I came across in a previous consultation in Australia.

The B2B firm is headquartered on the east coast of Australia and serves clients located in several countries around the South Pacific and South East Asia regions. Therefore, I had to develop a plan to allow their social media team to engage with social followers in different time zones during business hours.

The first step is working out the extremes of each time zone, taking daylight savings time into account: The east coast of Australia sits in the middle of the time zone between the furthest west country, Thailand, and the furthest east country, New Zealand. Here's how it looks over each 12 month period from April to April:

Standard Time (Apr – Sep):
Thailand -3hrs ← Aust. East Coast → +2hrs New Zealand

Daylight Savings (Sep – Apr):
Thailand -3hrs ← Aust. East Coast → +3hrs New Zealand

This means content should be scheduled at a time that ensures the target audience in all regions are exposed to said content during business hours on the Australian east coast. As a result, any immediate user comments and questions can be responded to in real-time.

Therefore, there are two possible options that can optimise the posting schedule for each time zone:

- Post once a day at a single optimal time and reassess the optimal times regularly.

Or

- Post more than once a day with content aimed at the specific times and interests of each region (social media management tools can be used to only show content to specific countries at specific times).

At first thought, the second option would produce better results in terms of overall engagement but the choice will ultimately come down to available time and content. My recommendation to my client, therefore, was to begin posting once on each social media platform after lunch at 1pm every day, except on Twitter, which would have tweets and retweets at regular intervals during Australian business hours. When the team are comfortable running this initial plan, they can then increase their engagement to include more location-targeted posts.

Now in charge of completed social media profiles and having a good grasp on what your potential clients are interested in (and when to reach them), the next item on your checklist is what kind of content you will produce and share.

Thirds, Fourths, Fifths, or 10% - Who Rules? – Rule Of Thirds

Not to be confused with the better-known photography rule, the 'rule of thirds' encourages a more well-rounded social media content strategy to both promote the brand and better engage with social media communities. The rule states that a third of social content aims to promote the business, a third of social content should share ideas and stories from thought leaders in your industry, and the final third of social content should be based on personal interactions and building a personal brand. In other words, published social media content should be made up of:

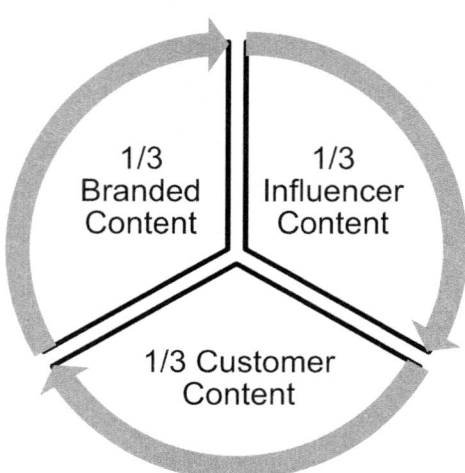

Exhibit 3.19   Social Media Rule of Thirds

Initially, this can be achieved by posting at least one piece of branded, influencer, and customer content every day as scheduled in your editorial calendar. Going forward, each type of content can be increased based on post performance and available resources. I'll use a few tweets to illustrate each of the three content types.

Cisco @Cisco · 19h
An eager spirit makes Cisco employee @cbarnabe the epitome of Our People Deal: cs.co/6011Bk76l #WeAreCisco

Exhibit 3.20   Cisco Branded Tweet

Adobe @Adobe · 9h
Simple, clean and beautiful. Designer @andrewcouldwell on what went into Adobe Portfolio: bit.ly/1QOUnR1

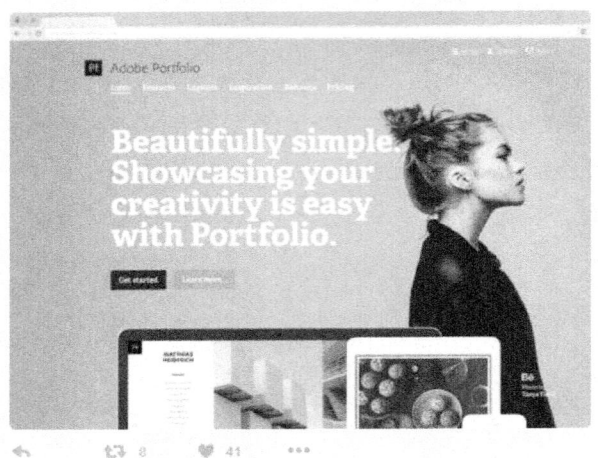

8   41   •••

Exhibit 3.21　　　Adobe Influencer Tweet

Pinned Tweet
Intel @intel · 17h
.@markmcmorris just brought @XGames fans a great run on Slopestyle w/Intel tech and real-time data. See it here!

108   156   •••

Exhibit 3.22　　　Intel Customer Tweet

You may have heard similar support for a rule of fourths or fifths and even a 10% rule, where you only talk about yourself one time out of every ten posts. The problem I have with reducing the number of times you post content about your business is that while you may be very knowledgeable about many things, you are definitely an expert on one: you. And since this is a social media strategy geared towards B2B companies, it makes sense that you want to talk about what you do a good proportion of the time; whether it be promotional or otherwise.

Note: I first became aware of the social media rule of thirds from a blog post on Hootsuite; who incidentally operate my social media management tool of choice but we'll save this discussion for Chapter 6.

CHAPTER THREE ACTION STEPS:

❑ If you haven't selected four social media platforms yet, read the best practice guides and determine if you have the required resources to implement them.

❑ If you have selected four social media platforms, make notes of the best practices for future reference when it comes time to create content.

❑ Decide on the username convention for your brand that will be used across all social media platforms.

❑ Update your profiles with brief yet informative bio text, a website link, and consistent branded profile images.

❑ Join communities on LinkedIn, Twitter, Facebook, YouTube, Google+, SlideShare, Pinterest, and Instagram to find out who your target audience is and what content they like to consume.

❑ Make a table of the five key content types that are gratifying for each audience segment and use this table to make a list of the five key content types that are gratifying across all audience segments.

❑ If applicable, note the different time zones of your audience across your serviced region. Aim to schedule your posts within these time zones to engage everyone.

❑ Make sure everyone involved in the social media content creation and scheduling process understands and follows the rule of thirds. This means posting equal amounts of branded, influencer, and customer content as scheduled in your editorial calendar.

PART II

Content with Content

Chapter 4 – Creating Content
Chapter 5 – Editorial Calendar
Chapter 6 – Daily Social Media Management

This section deals with content. You've got your audience interests pinned down. Now it's time to curate and create content that aligns with these interests. But where to begin?

You could go out with guns blazing and post all sorts of branded and non-branded content, trying to hit every one of those interests. But as you'll see from Chapter 4, having a goal for your content and creating engaging posts according to your own unique set of branding standards makes consistent and effective social media activity achievable.

To further aid consistency, an editorial calendar details you and your associate's daily social media posts, keeping everyone involved aware of what has and what hasn't been scheduled for each platform. Chapter 5 presents an example editorial calendar for your reference and discusses the advantages of supporting the editorial calendar with a one-page, colour-coded cheat sheet.

To further further aid consistency, you'll be happy to discover how inexpensive social media management tools reduce the time and effort required to find and schedule content across all of your chosen social media platforms. Find out how in Chapter 6.

In case you haven't guessed already, I'm a big believer that consistency equals success on social media. Churchill got it right when he said, "Continuous effort—not strength or intelligence—is the key to unlocking our potential."

CHAPTER FOUR:
CREATING CONTENT

Either write something worth reading or do something worth writing about.

- BEN FRANKLIN

CHAPTER CONTENTS

- Types of Content
- Have a Goal for Content
- Content Style Guide
- Content Bank

Up to this point you should have a list of your target audience interests and the intention to post branded, influencer, and customer content an equal 33.3% of the time. Save for having a goal for all that you post on social media, your entire content strategy is almost in the bag. Knowing all the various types of content you can create for each social media platform beforehand makes goal setting easier.

No Skills, No Time, No Resources, No Problem! – Types of Content

The type of content you create will always depend on your available resources. It would be challenging—near impossible—to construct eye-catching infographics, for example, without professional design software (although I've seen a few impressive infographics made using PowerPoint). Similarly, writing long blog posts would be challenging to someone with modest writing experience and little time to learn.

Let's dive right in and discuss the possible types of content you can create for sharing on social media:

- Ideal for micro-blogging sites like Twitter but also handy for short posts on LinkedIn and Facebook, company updates and announcements between 100 and 200 words deliver a lot of value within very short snippets of information.
  Required resources: Set aside a couple of minutes at most to write and schedule these from within your

social media management tool, giving you a lot of bang for your buck.

- Articles around 700 words were the bread and butter of almost every blogger since blogs began. Most still write this length of post but readers are increasingly avoiding these traditional blog posts in favour of their shorter or longer cousins.
  Required resources: Chose an idea for an engaging article and split it up into an intro, three paragraphs and a conclusion. The alternative is to write a list ("Top 10 …", "10 Ways to …") article, probably the most read type of blog post online.

- Articles exceeding 1,500 words are generally well-researched and contain quality images and links. They're usually categorised as evergreen since their content remains relevant for a long time after the publish date.
  Required resources: You'll need at least a couple of weeks to build one long blog post in addition to the time needed to upload the article, complete with optimised images and functioning links.

- There's no set guidelines for eBook length or content. That's why you'll find eBooks for almost every topic on the internet, with varying levels of quality.
  Required resources: If you thought two weeks to

write a long article was excessive, writing an eBook requires much more effort. The effort pays off in a big way, though, since giving away a value-laden eBook in return for a client's contact information is a great way to boost lead generation.

- Of course, images are the only way you'll use Pinterest and Instagram, but images should be included in pretty much every post on LinkedIn, Facebook, Google+, and Twitter also. Posts with attached images attract much more engagement than text-only posts.
  Required resources: It's easy to maintain a bank of ready-to-go images you can use in your social media posts and they take nanoseconds to upload.

- Videos are not just for YouTube. When Facebook started supporting images, they overtook text-only posts in terms of user popularity and engagement. And the same thing happened to images when videos started showing up on Facebook.
  Required resources: Videos demand a lot of resources to plan, shoot, edit, and upload. There's also no exact science to shooting share-worthy videos, meaning you could get five million views or you could get just five. If you do have the resources, however, I recommend using them because having even just one viral success could make all the difference in hitting your objectives.

- Podcasts are basically videos you listen to instead of watch. Perhaps I'm oversimplifying podcasting a wee bit. Like a powerful presentation, podcasts take interesting content and split it up into several parts of a longer series but can easily stand up on their own.

  Required resources: If you have a lot to say but no time to write it all down and publish as an article, why not record it instead? Your number one priority for podcasting is using quality audio equipment including a noise-cancelling microphone.

- Infographics are perfect for sharing because of the way they take often-boring data and present them in a way that's very appealing. The trouble with a lot of infographics online today, however, is that they are poorly executed; either because the data didn't really require an infographic or a digital marketer cared more about getting backlinks than putting effort into designing the infographic.

  Required resources: Add the time taken to research some trustworthy data to the time taken to put the data into graphical format along with background designs and a general theme and you understand why infographics are so time-consuming. If you can afford it, though, I suggest creating infographics because their capacity to be shared on social media and increase both brand awareness and website traffic is tremendous.

- Presentations are a great way to tell an educational story in an interesting and easily-digestible way. Impart your wisdom with a striking collection of unique fonts, compelling copy, and high-resolution images.

  Required resources: SlideShare accepts common file formats like PowerPoint, Canva, and freeware applications, so keep it simple but not so simple that you resort to using the basic template designs. Include plenty of images and keep text to a minimum; the average 14 slides of 25 words on each slide equals just 350 words. Think of it like entering a 25-words-or-less competition on every slide.

Setting Goals for Content

What do you want your content to do? Entertain your readers? Solve a problem? Educate your readers? Or perhaps you want to get your ideas across and foster discussion?

If your goal is lead generation, have you made your content as simple as it can possibly be for potential leads to get in touch with you? If it takes more than a few clicks or entering too much information, simplify it. You can always seek more information later once potential leads have entered the conversion funnel.

If your goal is client retention, you must post content that validates their decision to work with you. That means highlighting the best features of your services and products as well as building your reputation as an authority through educational content. If done successfully, you will have more opportunities for cross-selling and up-selling.

If your goal is brand awareness, your content has to strike such a chord in the people who consume said content that they feel compelled to share it with their friends. Word of mouth has always been and will likely continue to be the most powerful form of marketing. As a result, make sure your content is so good that your fans look good when they share it and make sure your content is easy to be shared.

Whatever your goals are, always think of how it will stimulate all who consume it to either contact you or share it with those who may want to contact you.

Contingency Planning for Your Brand's Voice – Content Style Guide

Okay so you've decided on the type of content you want to create and you have a goal for your content. You can go ahead and start creating and posting, right? Well what happens when you no longer have the time to create content or, knock on wood, your current social media specialist can no longer continue in their role and you need to up-skill a current employee or bring an intern on board to take the reins?

Whether it happens to your business or not, it makes sense to create a content style guide to keep all employees responsible for content creation and posting on the same page. It also works as a contingency plan if you need to quickly train a new employee, social media specialist or intern in the future.

In your content style guide, it is essential that you break down all the elements unique to your branding into individual segments. This ensures your content remains effective no matter who is in charge of its creation and your social media followers consume the consistently great posts they're used to seeing. It doesn't mean holding your social media associate's hand through every status update and tweet. It's more like having a secure set of basic standards for content that doesn't stray from your company values, brand style and business goals. And because it works in this way, your social media associate can work independently in line with your guidelines, even while posting and responding on the various platforms.

While I suggest you have some flexibility with regards to your social media activity, the foundations of your style guide should include the following items:

- **Font**
  Any font embedded in images should follow the same consistent font styles used in your other

marketing material. This includes line spacing and bulleting/numbering formats.

- **Tone of Voice**
  Ensure a consistent tone, voice, spelling, grammar, and language is maintained. In general, a friendly tone with uniform use of pronouns (you, we, us, our, etc.) and commonly used social media expressions/exclamations is the norm. For B2B specifically, aim for an authoritative yet humble tone—displaying confidence in your expertise but never appearing arrogant—and try to avoid slang terms.

- **Imagery**
  Your images should always align with your brand's style and personality. This includes using a consistent colour palette plus deciding if and where you will place your brand's logo on images.

- **Profile**
  Your cover photos should be visually attractive, with something in the image that makes your page identifiable to users immediately. The profile image on IBM's Facebook page is a good example of this.

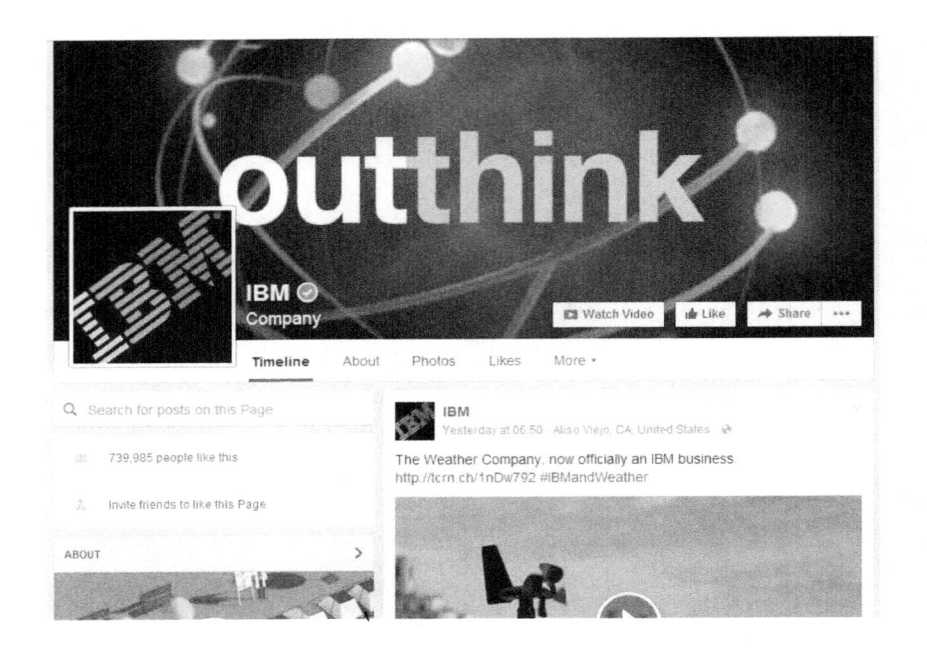

Exhibit 4.1   IBM Facebook Page

Character Length

Kevan Lee of buffersocial suggests (and backed by good research) that the optimal length of a Facebook post should be less than 40 characters. I agree with Lee's suggestion that fewer characters increase engagement but there will be exceptions depending on the topic. And switching it up every now and then keeps things interesting. What's more, it can be super hard to stay within the limit—even 140-character tweets are challenging!

Here's what 76 characters looks like:

Exhibit 4.2   IBM Facebook Post

Looks pretty short already, right? Try introducing this video in an engaging way using just 40 characters, 12 of which already being earmarked for a branded hashtag. Forget about it! It simply doesn't make sense to set such strict boundaries for social media content. View these best practices more as a guideline.

Therefore, I suggest simply trying to keep posts as short as possible. Fun images and videos could contain around 40 characters. Questions and announcements could contain around 40 characters. But they will likely be much longer;

especially when posting status updates, company news and product info.

Image Dimensions

Like Instagram, there is an optimal image size that will ensure the highest image quality when viewed across all devices. Here's a list of the relevant image dimensions for LinkedIn, SlideShare, Facebook, Twitter, Google+, Pinterest, and Instagram:

- LinkedIn profile photo: 400 x 400 pixels
- LinkedIn cover photo: 646 x 220 pixels
- LinkedIn image: 800 x 800 pixels
- SlideShare page: 1024 x 768 pixels
- Facebook cover photo: 851 x 315 pixels
- Facebook app thumbnail: 111 x 74 pixels
- Minimum Facebook photo post: 504 x 504 pixels
- Twitter header photo: 1500 x 500 pixels
- Minimum tweeted image: 440 x 220 pixels
- Google+ cover photo: 1080 x 608 pixels
- Pinterest profile photo: 160 x 165 pixels
- Pinterest pinned image: 735 x 1102 pixels
- Instagram photo: 1080 x 1080 pixels

If you'd prefer a one-page cheat sheet 'The 2016 Social Media Image Sizes Guide' below explains the best image sizes for each social network and the best image types to use. Jamie Spencer of MakeAWebsiteHub.com has listed every major social media platform on this updated infographic; perfect for social media image optimization in 2016 and beyond.

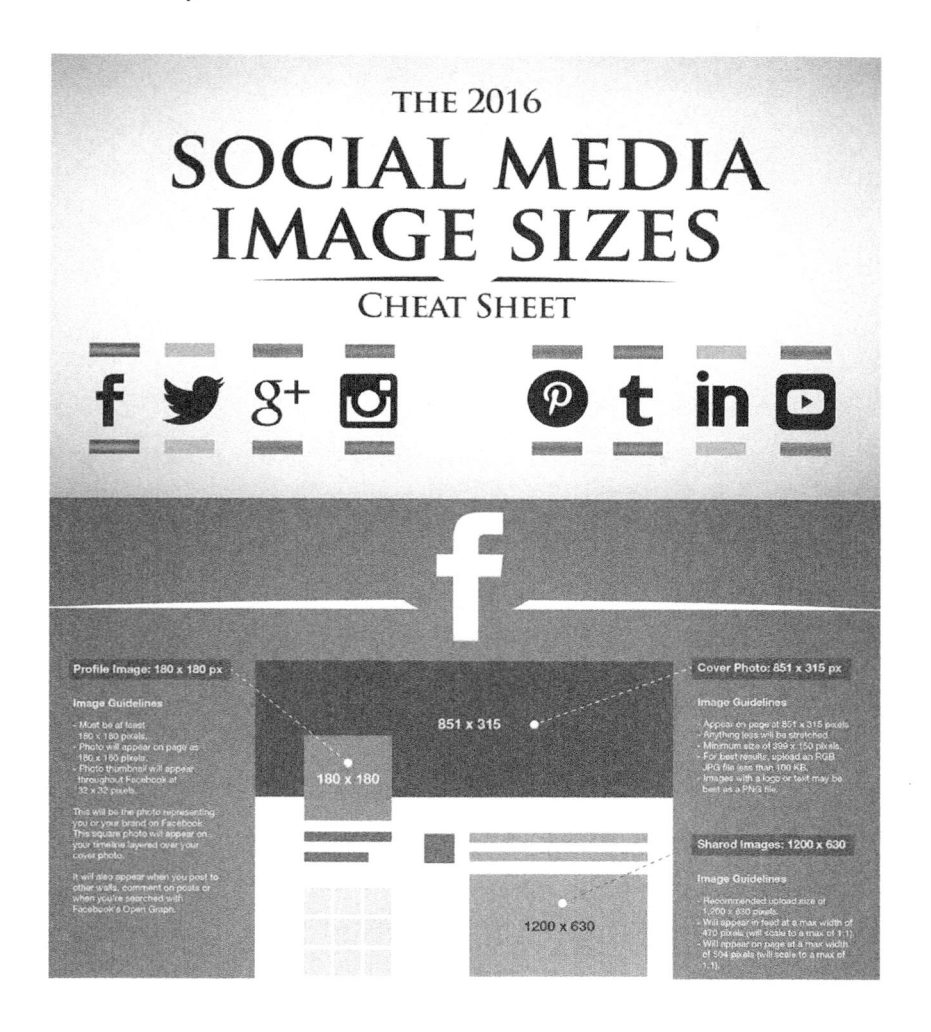

Exhibit 4.3   2016 Social Media Image Sizes Cheat Sheet

This is a handy reference to keep in your bookmarks or print it off and keep it close at hand any time you're posting an image for your social media profiles.

Maintain A Strong Content Bank and You'll Avoid This Common Mistake

Having a folder packed with share-worthy content is priceless to any business. Why? Because the amount of time your social media associate will save on a daily, weekly, monthly, and yearly basis is phenomenal thanks to an initial period of effort—we're talking about days of productivity that can be better spent on other marketing activities over a whole year, not just a few hours.

I don't want to give you a heart attack at this point with talk of creating an entire year's worth of original content for social media. Adding content you already have at your disposal—both old and new—in smaller batches up to a month in advance is a good way to maintain a strong content bank as well as avoid content fatigue.

Like other chapters in Part II, your content bank fits neatly alongside your editorial calendar. Possibly the most time-consuming and often frustrating task in social media for B2B companies is curating content. Having an entire bank of content at your fingertips makes it a hell of a lot easier to enter into your editorial calendar. As a result, short bursts of making deposits into your content bank can result in months of engaging social media posts all ready to be scheduled as listed in your calendar.

As you'll read in the section 'Content vs. Interests' in Chapter 5, I suggest cross-referencing the interests of your target audience segments into a master list of the top five interests. These top five will then guide your daily content strategy. To make things easier for your social media associate, then, I recommend maintaining specified folders for each content type in your content bank rather than three folders for each segment in the rule of thirds; and certainly rather than a huge unorganised list of random images.

Having generated a content bank personally, I reckon you need to set aside two full days to fill your folder with enough content for a month's worth of social media posts. This means adding an evenly distributed number of images into each of the five 'interest' folders. As your folders begin to fill up, you'll discover which interests have a shortage of content. Much better to find out any deficiencies during these two days than waiting until the day of posting and you end up scrambling to find something interesting to post on that day.

I suggested adding older content to your bank. This is because old content can be repurposed quite effectively on social media platforms. I'm sure you've seen Facebook posts titled, 'Throwback Thursday' or something similar. And as I showed in the best practices for Facebook, older images can turn an ok post into a captivating milestone.

And it's not just images you'll store in your content bank (otherwise it'd be an image bank!). Dedicated YouTube and

Facebook videos can be stored also. Figures prove that videos uploaded to Facebook directly draw more views than those embedded from YouTube so aim to create videos purposely designed for publishing on each platform. And if you have interesting videos up to 15 seconds long, make sure you add them to your Instagram content bank. In the same manner as videos, infographics are perfect for sharing on Pinterest as are presentations for LinkedIn and SlideShare.

When the time comes for you or your social media associate to schedule content in your editorial calendar, a quick search through your content bank will flag ideal content for each day and platform. Sometimes, you'll have images and other content that can be posted across various platforms or several posts. But to make content scheduling a breeze for anyone involved in the process, you'll need a proper file system.

How to Make Content Open and Easy to Find – The File System

Put on your administrator hat for a few minutes, we're going to talk about filing. I know how easy is it to save files on your computer and then not remember where you put them. I've also worked in companies where employees maintain folders across different servers, or worse, saving them on their desktop, making it impossible for others to find them (and I include myself in this group). Going forward with social media, however, we'll need to decide on a proper filing system for your content bank.

As you'll read in the following chapter, I have described the advantages of using an editorial calendar—an Excel spreadsheet that lists daily social media content. The editorial calendar includes a column titled, "ASSETS & LOCATION". This is where you will enter the location of any images and/or other files to be included within that post. As a result, anyone involved in managing your social media profiles can open the editorial calendar and locate the intended media file and offer any suggestions; or if the person in charge of posting your content opens the editorial calendar, they will be able to locate the files quickly.

From experience, I find it a lot easier to have a single folder named "Social Media". The only prerequisite for this folder's location is that it can be accessed by all social media stakeholders in your company. Within this folder is nothing more than a list of folders; one for each of your social media profiles and one each for your calendars and content bank. For example, you would have six folders titled, "Content Bank", "Editorial Calendar", "Facebook", "Google Plus", "LinkedIn", and "Twitter" if you only used these four platforms. No other content should appear in the "Social Media" folder. You will then keep specific content within each of your social media platform folders.

With regards to file name conventions, I have found that

dates rather than image subject matter work best. For example, if you have reserved an image for posting on Facebook on August 21, 2016, then you would simply save the image in the Facebook folder titled "20160821". Why put the date backwards? This means the image files will be listed in your folders in correct numerical order; again, this makes them easier to find.

Note: This file naming convention is acceptable for social media images because each platform will host the images and change the file name to gobbledegook. Images posted on your website should follow the more SEO-friendly format with descriptive keywords and your brand name. This makes your images more likely to show in the results when users search online.

CHAPTER FOUR ACTION STEPS:

☐ Take a good look at your currently available resources and, based on what you discover, decide on the type of content you want to create.

☐ Decide what you want your content to do; whether it's to entertain, solve a problem, educate, or get your ideas across.

☐ Create a content style guide to keep all your social media stakeholders on the same page. Break down all the elements unique to your branding into individual segments. Ask yourself, is it clear enough that any new employees can quickly understand its contents?

☐ Practice writing short posts and calculating the length. How well can you stay within, say, a 100-character limit when composing a tweet?

☐ Open a new folder in one of your shared servers and start adding share-worthy images, videos, and presentations that would make great posts across your chosen platforms.

☐ Decide on a proper filing system for your content bank. Ensure all social media stakeholders have access to the necessary folders—including permissions to add and edit files within. Add a rule for consistent file name conventions in your style guide to maintain a clean and easy-access inventory.

CHAPTER FIVE:
EDITORIAL CALENDAR

Plan your work for today and every day, then work your plan.
- MARGARET THATCHER

CHAPTER CONTENTS

- Content vs. Interests
- Cheat Sheet
- Detailed Editorial Calendar

This chapter packs a powerful punch. In Chapter 5, like Rocky V, you'll mature your protégé into a real title contender with the stamina to throw jabs left and right for the full 12 rounds. Put another way, your social media strategy will develop alongside a dependable editorial calendar to ensure you post daily content for at least the next 12 months—and deliver a knockout blow every now and then!

Enough boxing analogies, let's talk about planning daily social media activity. A daily plan is important in order to maintain consistency over time; especially if results are not immediately forthcoming and you begin to lack the motivation to keep posting and tracking. That's why I believe this chapter may be the most important of all. If you take away nothing else, I hope I can convince you of the significance of creating an editorial calendar.

An editorial calendar with a set of daily topics will enhance ongoing engagement on social media and ensure each profile continues to uphold a consistent publishing schedule and brand voice. The editorial calendar will also streamline the social media strategy by discovering the optimal days and times for future publishing and engagement.

It all begins by creating a list of audience interests, with an outline of the specific topics you'll post laid out in a table. This is where some flexibility comes in.

Content vs. Interests

Following the example of brands like Virgin who regularly post their latest 'hot jobs' on Tuesdays and often posts vintage photographs on Thursdays, your content should fall into one of five categories to be posted on specific days of the week. By the way, if you're looking for a brand—B2B or B2C—to emulate on social media, I suggest you follow Virgin.

This will make content creation and scheduling more consistent and less time consuming. Similarly, your audience will learn what type of content you are likely to post on certain days and see you as an authority. For example, if you hear about an upcoming event in your industry, you can post it on the day you normally post industry news. Your followers, meanwhile, will know to check in with your profile on that same day each week to get the latest news in your industry.

The content you post should include the top five audience interests determined during your target audience research. If you'll recall from my earlier example about the travel company, the top five audience interests I found were Industry and Your Brand, Offers, Travel, Tips & Tricks, and Entertainment.

I then advise you to assign each category to a different day of the week, keeping in mind what topics your audience will enjoy on specific days—industry news on Mondays and

Industry	Tips & Tricks	Offers	Events	Entertainment
- Industry News	- Instructional Tips	- Campaigns	- Sports Events	- Entertaining
- Expert Views	- Videos	- Offers	- Music Events	- Quotes
- Interviews	- Community Groups	- Competitions	- Cultural Events	- Pets & Animals
- Partner Brands	- Getting To Know The ___	- Questions	- Festivals	- Public Figures
- Product Info	- Culture	- Polls	- Group Travel	- Inspirational
- Exclusive Brand News	- Health & Beauty	- International Days	- Outdoor Activities	- TV Shows & Movies
- Milestones		- Shopping	- Things To Do	- Food & Recipes
			- Attractions	
			- Holidays & Seasonal	

Exhibit 5.1 Content Types Split into Daily Categories

entertainment on Fridays, for example—and aim to feature people any visual content where possible. Exhibit 5.1 shows how this would look in a clear table.

The Nail-It-to-Your-Wall Cheat Sheet

The table of daily categories like the one shown in Exhibit 5.1 flows neatly into developing your social media cheat sheet—your guiding light in consistent engagement. The social media cheat sheet hangs on the wall and provides a quick overview of daily content types and schedule for each social media platform, and is used in alignment with the detailed editorial calendar.

The cheat sheet is arranged so that anyone can grasp what's meant to be posted on any given day with just a second's glance. Exhibit 5.2 shows how a 5-day social media cheat sheet would look for the example travel company. As you can see, it uses an easily-identifiable layout with sections for day of the week, content interest category, social media platform, and when content is to be scheduled along with any profile maintenance.

The success of the entire layout relies on the unique colour coordination used in conjunction with the table of interest you made in the previous step. Even from a distance that makes reading the text impossible, you can still determine the type of content to be posted on any given day.

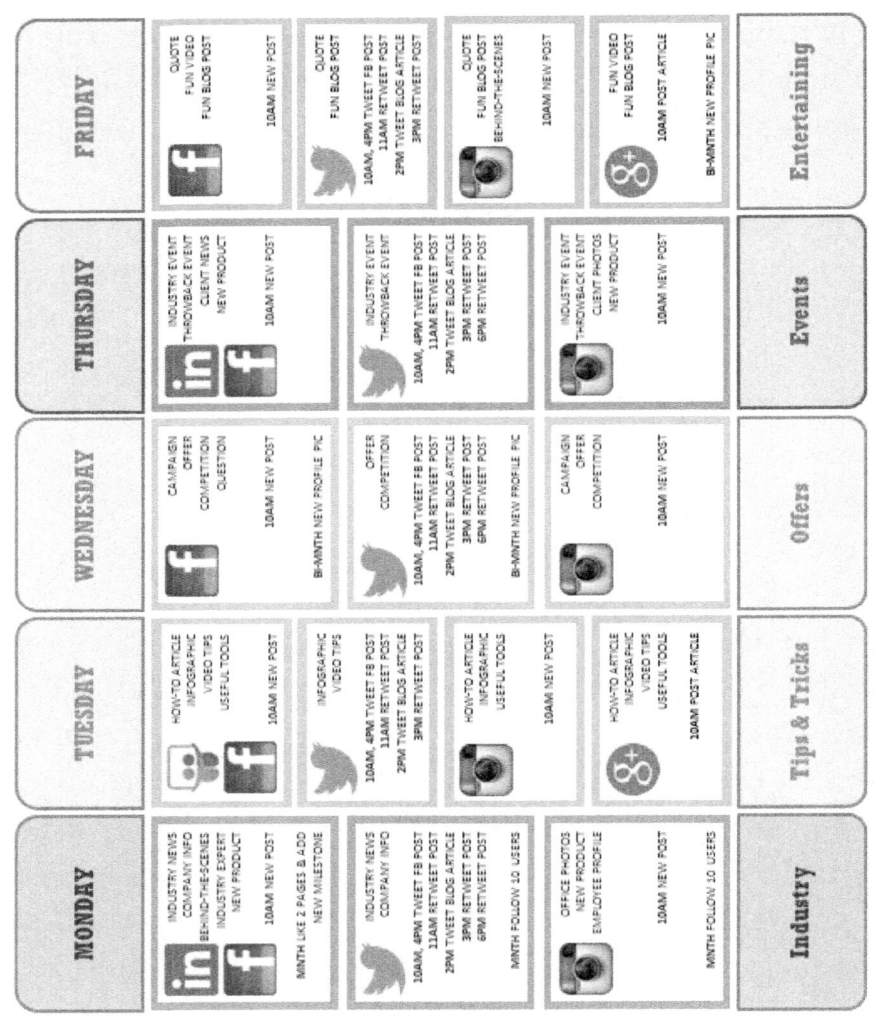

Image source: Author.

Exhibit 5.2 Social Media 5-Day Cheat Sheet Wall Chart

Here's a detailed explanation of how the 5-day cheat sheet is arranged by day, colour, platform, schedule, and interests:

- **Monday**

Blue = Industry and Your Brand

- o Facebook – Post about industry and brand news at 10am. Once a month, like two new pages and add a new milestone.
- o LinkedIn – Post about industry and brand news at 10am.
- o Twitter – Tweet the Facebook post at 10am and schedule it again for 4pm. Schedule a tweet linking to an industry-related blog article to publish at 2pm. Schedule fan retweets to publish at 11am, 3pm, and 6pm. Once a month, follow 10 new profiles.
- o Instagram – Post a new image at 10am showing off your brand, product, or staff.

- **Tuesday**

  Orange = Tips & Tricks

  - o SlideShare – Post an educational SlideShare presentation at 10am.
  - o Facebook – Post a link to the SlideShare presentation at 10am.
  - o Twitter – Tweet the Facebook post at 10am and schedule it again for 4pm. Schedule a tweet linking to an educational blog article to publish at 2pm. Schedule fan retweets to publish at 11am and 3pm.
  - o Instagram – Post a new image at 10am of an interesting and handy product.

- o Google+ – Post a link to the SlideShare presentation at 10am.

- **Wednesday**
  Green = Offers
  - o Facebook – Post a new promotion or competition at 10am. Once every two months, upload a new profile picture.
  - o Twitter – Tweet the Facebook post at 10am and schedule it again for 4pm. Schedule a tweet linking to an industry-related blog article to publish at 2pm. Schedule fan retweets to publish at 11am, 3pm, and 6pm. Once every two months, upload a new profile picture.
  - o Instagram – Post a new image about the promotion or competition (prize) at 10am.

- **Thursday**
  Red = Events
  - o Facebook – Post about an industry or brand event at 10am.
  - o LinkedIn – Post about an industry or brand event at 10am.
  - o Twitter – Tweet the Facebook post at 10am and schedule it again for 4pm. Schedule a tweet linking to an industry-related blog article to publish at 2pm. Schedule fan retweets to publish at 11am,

3pm, and 6pm.

- ○ Instagram – Post a new image about an industry or brand event at 10am.

- **Friday**
  Aqua = Entertainment
  - ○ Facebook – Post an entertaining video or inspiring quote at 10am.
  - ○ Twitter – Tweet the Facebook post at 10am and schedule it again for 4pm. Schedule a tweet linking to an industry-related blog article to publish at 2pm. Schedule fan retweets to publish at 11am and 3pm.
  - ○ Instagram – Post an inspiring quote or entertaining image at 10am.
  - ○ Google+ – Post an entertaining video or inspiring quote at 10am.

Remember that this is just an example for a B2B/B2C travel company. You will have a very different looking cheat sheet complete with any interests, colour scheme, images, layout, etc. you wish.

And if you aim to increase your social activity to include weekend posts, simply add Saturday and Sunday to your cheat sheet. I suggest keeping your weekend post practices light in terms of both quantity and type. Exhibit 5.3 shows

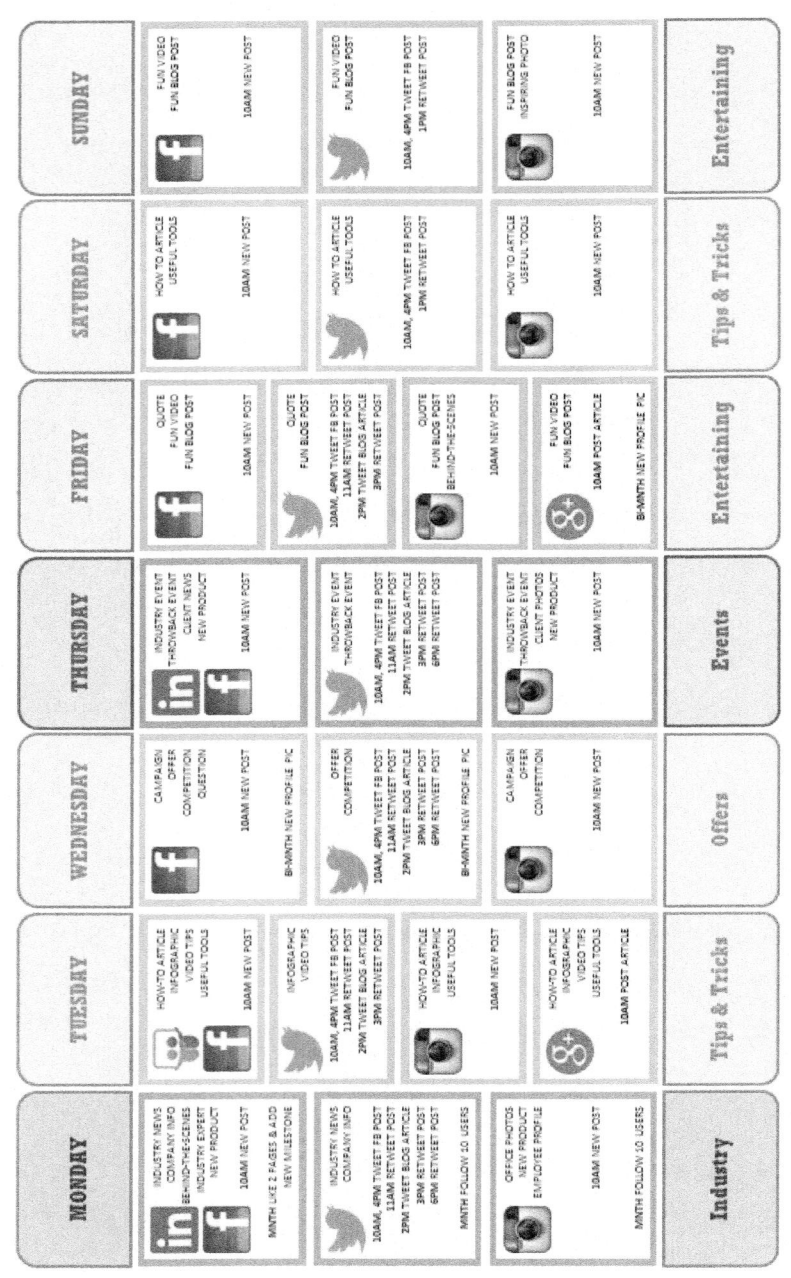

Image source: Author.

Exhibit 5.3   Social Media 7-Day Cheat Sheet Wall Chart

you what a 7-day cheat sheet would look with the extra weekend days. You'll notice I would devote Saturday posts to anything travel-related and Sunday posts to entertaining content like Wednesday and Friday, respectively.

The Simple Yet Detailed Editorial Calendar

If your cheat sheet is your guiding light for consistent engagement, your editorial calendar is how you follow that light; basically ensuring you continue on your quest one step at a time.

The detailed editorial calendar makes it far easier to create and schedule posts in advance and includes sections for:

- **PUBLISH DATE**
  Enter the date you expect to schedule this post. Excel should automatically change your date to its pre-formatted version after you press Enter, helping you maintain a consistent format in this column.

- **TIME**
  Enter the time you expect to schedule this post. This should be in parallel with what you entered in your cheat sheet.

- **PLATFORM**
  Enter the date you expect to publish this post. You can pre-enter these platforms into a drop-

down list using Excel's Data Validation tool to make scheduling quicker.

- **CONTENT TYPE**
The content type (colour coded) is nothing more than a short statement describing what the post is or contains.

- **AUTHOR**
Enter the initials of any and all social media associates credited with creating this post.

- **DRAFT TEXT**
Enter the text you plan to use for this post. Also include any hashtags and mentions. Your social media management tool will shorten any links you wish to use in your text, while any links you plan on using to auto-populate posts on Facebook and Google+ do not need to be entered here.

- **LENGTH**
This uses the Excel formula *=LEN(F#)* where F is the column titled "DRAFT TEXT" and # is the row number of the corresponding post. The length will help you draft shorter posts and make sure you stay within Twitter's 140-character limit.

- **ASSETS & LOCATION**
Enter the file location of any content you plan on

using for this post. If there's you'll use to auto-populate posts on Facebook and Google+, enter it here to prevent it giving a false text length.

- **STATUS**
  Enter the status of this post. I normally have three statuses: 1) Not Started – none or a few of the entries for this post have been completed but the post has not been scheduled; 2) Scheduled – when you have scheduled this post in your social media management tool; and 3) Published – when a post has been published. You can pre-enter these statuses into a drop-down list using Excel's Data Validation tool.

- **RETWEET**
  This column is simply a reminder to retweet posts as scheduled in your cheat sheet. This is useful because retweets are not given their own row in the editorial calendar to save space and because they don't require draft text or assets.

As you can see in Exhibit 5.4, the colour codes in the Cheat Sheet correspond to the colour codes in the detailed editorial calendar—except for the monthly and bi-monthly tasks such as updating profile images and following other profiles, which are coloured in grey in my example.

NOTE: My apologies if you are reading this book in

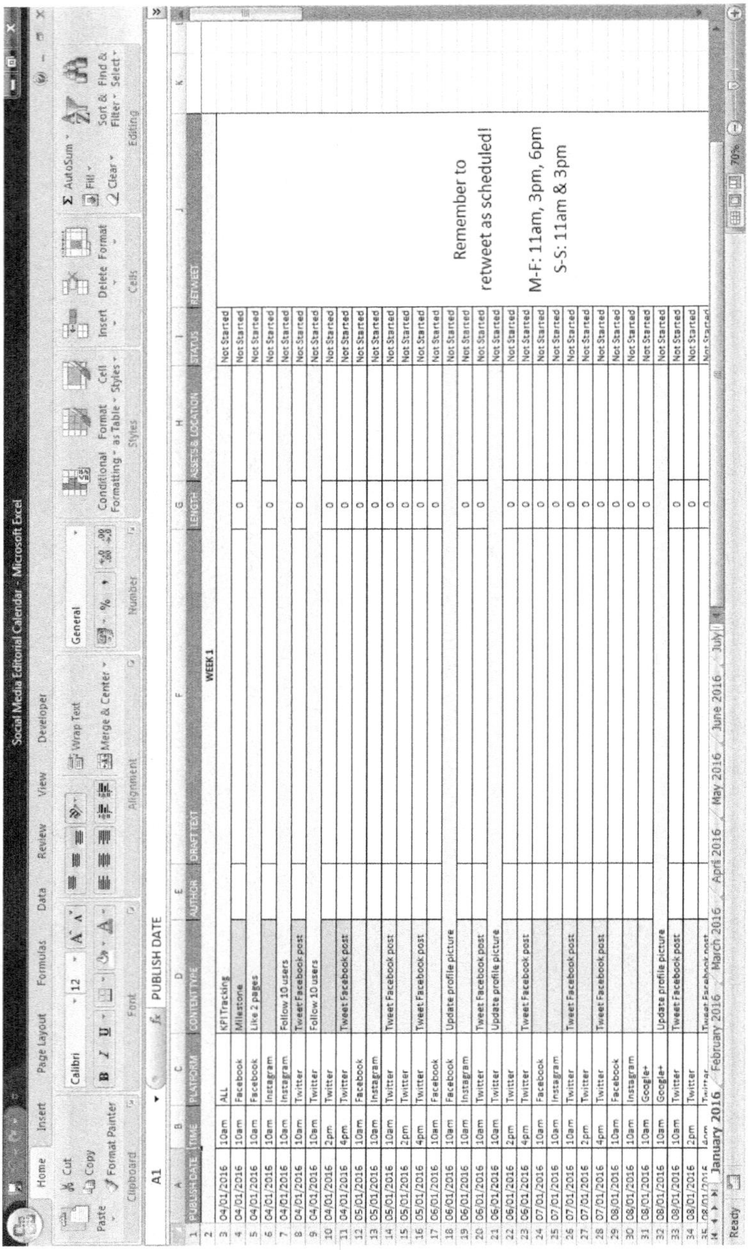

Image source: Author.

Exhibit 5.4   Social Media Editorial Calendar

black and white. I understand that you may not be able to match the colour codes in my cheat sheet and editorial calendar. I hope you can see the different shades of grey, however.

The chapter you have just digested is brief yet powerful. Apart from cramming your content bank full of awesome images and videos, creating your cheat sheet and editorial calendar will be the most time consuming part of your social media strategy.

But like your content bank, the initial resources put into creating your editorial calendar will actually save you time in the long run while increasing accountability, consistency, and capacity for tracking results.

CHAPTER FIVE ACTION STEPS:

❑ Make a five by two table like the one shown in Exhibit 5.1. Start by typing a different audience interest in each cell of row 1 in the order of the days of the week starting with Monday—ignore the weekend for the moment. Now format each of the cells in row 1 with a unique colour. Finally, add the types of content and various interests that fall under each daily category in row 2.

❑ Create a cheat sheet using graphics software of your choice. I made mine using PowerPoint. You may design your cheat sheet to look like mine, with unique colours to match the audience interest table and a box for every social media platform you plan to use. Or you can use your own unique style. Add the type of content you plan to post on each day and enter the approximate time the post will be published. Print and hang your cheat sheet where everyone can see it.

❑ Add Saturday and Sunday to your cheat sheet if you have the resources available. (This may need a slight tweak in design in order to make it print-friendly.)

❑ Create an editorial calendar Excel spreadsheet. Feel free to copy my layout or design your own. Use your cheat sheet to help design the layout and make sure you include columns for date, time, platform, content type, text, and assets. Add any other relevant columns you wish such as post status and text length calculator.

CHAPTER SIX:
DAILY SOCIAL MEDIA MANAGEMENT

The less unnecessary effort you put into learning, the more successful you'll be.
- TONY BUZAN

CHAPTER CONTENTS

- Social Media Management Tool Selection
- Finding Shareable Content
- Influencers

Managing Social Media Accounts

Research has found that B2B marketers use an average of six social media platforms. That means there are B2B superheroes out there juggling seven, eight, nine, or more social media accounts when it's possible that even just one of these platforms could consume the entire working week of a full-time marketer.

But lacking in superpowers, many B2B marketers turn to social media management tools for assistance. Before comparing three of the most popular social media management tools, it is necessary here to explain why these tools are useful; particularly to small businesses.

Social Media Management Tool Selection

A small business has many priorities to overcome in its quest to develop the business. Employees may already be too busy working on many important projects within the business to spend time collecting and scheduling content as well as keeping track of brand mentions and engaging with other users on social media. Social media management applications offer a number of benefits for social media marketers, including the ability to:

1. Manage the company's social media accounts from a single location, saving time spent logging into each platform.

2. Schedule content for publishing across selected

platforms.

3. Target users in specific locations and at certain times of the day.

4. Assign tasks to other employees.

5. Perform analysis of posts and monitor relevant keywords.

6. Generate reports to present to company stakeholders.

7. Send posts to upper management for evaluation before posting.

Hootsuite, Sprout Social, and Sendible are just three of the many available social media management tools on the internet. It wouldn't be efficient, or necessary, to compare every available tool in this book. The three applications selected have all received positive and negative reviews from past and current users.

Based on my review of user reviews when selecting a suitable tool for a previous client, the criteria I used to judge the three applications included, but were not limited to: the number of supported social media sites, ease of use, navigation, design and layout, customer support, price, and any unique additional features.

It is important to note that the digital industry is in continual development and improvement. While this is obviously a good thing for consumers, it does make documenting up-to-date information challenging. As a result, I have provided the most accurate features and prices of each tool at the time of writing, which may differ from the time you read this book and begin comparing these providers. My prediction, however, is that the three will maintain their order in terms of cost.

Hootsuite

Hootsuite is one of the top reviewed and most used management tools in existence, claiming user numbers beyond 10 million. It supports all the major social media platforms including LinkedIn, Facebook, Twitter, Google+, YouTube, Instagram, and Pinterest. It offers a wealth of tutorials and educational information on how to use Hootsuite as well as how to make the most of social media via its in-house educational platform: Hootsuite University.

Support for a selection of link-shortening options, including its own version, Ow.ly, make it easy for marketers to select the most effective tool for shortening links on posts. Finally, Hootsuite offers the most competitive pricing structure of the three management tools; including a free version that's open to any user from individual to large organisation.

Plan	Features
Free	• Free for one user • Up to 3 profiles • Email support • Basic analytics reports, basic message scheduling
Pro	• $10.99 per month for two users (if billed annually) • Up to 50 profiles • Helpdesk integration • One enhanced analytics report, advanced message scheduling, and advanced content suggestions.
Enterprise	• Price upon request. Up to 500,000 users • Unlimited profiles • Dedicated account rep • Unlimited enhanced analytics reports, advanced message scheduling, advanced content suggestions, training and enhanced technical support

Exhibit 6.1   Hootsuite Plan List[9]

The main weakness of using Hootsuite—based on reviewed user reviews—is navigation. Social media profiles, which means your Facebook profile, Twitter profile, etc.,

---

[9] https://hootsuite.com/plans

are organised into tabs, which makes them difficult to manage when trying to gain an overview of the current situation, and become even more so with additional profiles. Exhibit 6.1 displays the three plans available to new Hootsuite users.

Sprout Social

Sprout Social has also received many positive reviews from users based on three main benefits:

1. The live activity tracker shows real-time activity on each post to prevent more than one account manager working on the same post at the same time.

2. The 'ViralPost' feature analyses past audience engagement to suggest optimal post times.

3. It offers the most in-depth analysis of social media performance metrics of the three tools—important for tracking results and reporting your social media ROI to stakeholders.

Despite being the most expensive of the three, the most disappointing aspect of Sprout Social for users is the overly complicated layout, which has a steep learning curve to become skilled at using each feature. Exhibit 6.2 above displays the three plans available for new Sprout Social users.

Plan	Features
Deluxe	• $59 per user per month • Up to 10 profiles • Email support • Drafting, publishing & scheduling
Premium	• $99 per user per month • Up to 20 profiles • Helpdesk integration • Drafting, publishing & time-optimised scheduling
Team	• $500 for 3 users per month • Up to 30 profiles • 24/5 support • Drafting, advanced publishing permissions, time-optimised scheduling & custom branding

Exhibit 6.2 Sprout Social Plan List.[10]

Sendible

Sendible is the least well-known application of the three but is quickly gaining traction among users. Its Outlook-style layout is familiar to Microsoft Office users and therefore find it straightforward to navigate. This helps reduce the time required to master basic features for many users. In contrast to Hootsuite and Sprout Social, Sendible

---

[10] http://sproutsocial.com/pricing

supports email and SMS text messaging directly from the dashboard and the ability to automate replies based on a list of keywords within a user's question or comment.

Unfortunately, reviewers often gripe that although Sendible offers a wealth of features, it does not truly specialise in any one of those features.

Plan	Features
Startup	<ul><li>$59 per month</li><li>Up to 30 services</li><li>Email support</li><li>Up to 4 branded reports</li><li>2 team members</li></ul>
Business	<ul><li>$99 per month</li><li>Up to 60 services</li><li>Email support</li><li>Up to 8 branded reports</li><li>4 team members</li></ul>
Corporate	<ul><li>$139 per month</li><li>Up to 90 services</li><li>Live support</li><li>Up to 18 branded reports</li><li>6 team members</li></ul>

Exhibit 6.3   Sendible Plan List.[11]

---

[11] http://sendible.com/pricing/

Exhibit 6.3 displays three of the four plans available for new Sendible users—the fourth plan, Premium, is for very large organisations with large marketing departments and budgets and unlikely to be reading this book so I'll omit the Premium plan here.

Services, as shown in the Sendible price list, are defined as a service within a social media account. For example, a Twitter account can show the services, 'Comments', 'My Tweets', and 'Homefeed'.

Other social media management tools you may be interested in learning more about include Oktopost, Buffer, and SocialOomph.

And as a business owner or responsible employee, I'm sure you'll be eager to save on business expenses wherever possible. So I suggest you perform a Google search for any up-to-date discount codes you can use to save money on your chosen plan.

When It Takes Too Much Time to Find Shareable Content

The suggestions I made for tweeting and sharing content published by others only works if you find content worth sharing. It also only works for you and your available resources if you can find such content quickly. For this task, you need content sources.

Google is an obvious one. Type what you're looking for and click through to some of the results. What you won't get, though, is the full story on whether or not the blog post you've found is popular, trending or even recent; especially when the trend is towards hiding the actual publish date of blog articles to make them seem like new when in fact they could be several years old.

Thankfully, there are free websites dedicated to finding what's new and popular on the internet. I'll list a few of these here as a taster (along with their meta descriptions). Navigate your way through them and see if they flag interesting content that fits in with your message and if it's the type of content you'd like to share with your followers.

- BuzzFeed.com/trending – The top news stories from around the web. Find out what stories are trending right now on BuzzFeed.

- StumbleUpon.com – Free web-browser extension which acts as an intelligent browsing tool for discovering and sharing web sites.

- Hootsuite Suggested Content – By analyzing posting history and popular topics, it suggests a week's worth of messages containing relevant content that are ready to AutoSchedule.

- Digg.com – Digg is the homepage of the internet,

featuring the best articles, videos, and original content that the web is talking about right now.

- ContentGems.com – ContentGems scans hundreds of thousands of articles from the best online sources and presents you a stream of relevant and timely content.

- Alltop.com – Alltop categorizes all the top headlines from popular topics around the web.

- Scoop.it – Discover, curate and publish great content to get visibility online. Trusted by millions of professionals and thousands of companies.

- RightRelevance.com – Discover fresh relevant content to your interests, save interesting articles, follow influential experts, be the first to share soon-to-be viral content and much more.

- Trendspottr.com – Predicting emerging trends, viral content and key influencers for any topic. In real-time. From the social web.

And if you have a Facebook account, check out the Trending list on the right hand sidebar of your news feed to discover what the world is currently talking about. Similar tools dedicated to showing you what's trending are available on Twitter and Google+.

Influencers Who Boost Your Image Not Alienate Your Audience

Influencers are the social media users with enough clout to attract a long list of followers eager to engage with every post. Note that while there are influencers on every social media platform, you won't be able to follow them from your branded social media profiles except those on Twitter and Instagram. Apart from celebrities, influencers usually gain such popular status thanks to their unique talents, insights or imagery.

Influencers are valuable to businesses because if they share an image of themselves using your product (for B2C businesses) or they share content you have posted (for B2B and B2C) then you will receive a significant boost in followers, website visitors, clients, and customers. However, don't think of influencers as part of your advertising strategy. They already have a dedicated following and trying to coerce another user to modify their unique style to suit what you're trying to get across will likely alienate and upset their fans, damaging your brand and their reputation rather than enhance them.

Influencers can be found by searching Google for popular bloggers in your country. Click through to their Twitter and Instagram profiles to follow them if their posts align with what you do and your brand values.

At first, however, I recommend following 20 profiles on Twitter and Instagram. This will allow your live Twitter and Instagram streams on your chosen social media management tool to become populated with tweets that can be retweeted and images you can comment on.

CHAPTER SIX ACTION STEPS:

❑ Examine the costs and features of social media management tools. Compare Hootsuite, Sprout Social, Sendible and any other application you may find or have heard of and select the most appropriate one for you.

❑ Make a list of sources you will use to find shareable content.

❑ Make a list of 20 social media influencers in your industry for Twitter and Instagram—if each one is in your list of selected social media platforms—that you can start following today.

❑ Expand your influencer list to include those users you plan to follow in the future (Remember, don't follow everyone at once!). Add new influencers to the list as and when you come across them on social media or within your social media management tool.

PART III

Manage, Monitor & Market

Chapter 7 – Policy, Risk Management and Reputation
Chapter 8 – Monitoring and Reporting
Chapter 9 – Social Media Marketing

This section embraces Mark Zuckerberg's advice to keep up with the ever-changing digital landscape by taking risks. A willingness to take risks may be a spicy ingredient in the recipe for success but putting your brand's social reputation under threat without reason is unacceptable.

To mitigate negative outcomes, because you let user comments go unanswered or an enthusiastic undergrad engaged in an inappropriate conversation using your brand's profile, your company social media policy document will direct appropriate social media behaviour and help prevent a PR disaster.

Keeping social media followers on your side should be straightforward. Keeping stakeholders on your side should be equally simple. Chapter 8 explains how consistent tracking of your social media ROI and regular reporting to relevant stakeholders can be effortless with social media management tools.

Continuing with the theme of taking risks, Chapter 9 covers paid social media posts. Why are they risky? Well, let me ask, how many times have you clicked on a Facebook ad? If you're like me and other experienced users who are skilled in the art of ad-blindness, then the answer is never. And you begin to wonder if the budget could have been better spent elsewhere (AdWords perhaps?). But brands must be getting good results with social media marketing. This is what this chapter aims to uncover and discuss.

CHAPTER SEVEN:
POLICY, RISK MANAGEMENT AND REPUTATION

The biggest risk is not taking any risk. In a world that's changing really quickly, the only strategy that is guaranteed to fail is not taking risks.
- MARK ZUCKERBERG

CHAPTER CONTENTS

- Company Social Media Policy Document
- Engaging with Other Users
- Responding to Comments & Criticism

Not Having This Could Be Disastrous for Your Online Reputation – Company Social Media Policy Document

An official social media policy is important to document before starting your social media campaign because it will guide consistent communication standards for social media across the entire company and steer your marketing efforts in the right direction. Not having an official social media policy document could be disastrous for your online reputation and even land you in a spot of bother.

For instance, lacking guidelines for proper social media practice could result in accidental disclosure of company information, a violation of copyright or intellectual property, or other legal and business risks. In one well-known example, Nestlé were unprepared and ill-equipped to handle an attack by Greenpeace supporters when they organised a full-scale attack on the food giant's Facebook page, which seriously hurt Nestlé's reputation online. Your social media policy, then, should also include the necessary procedures for public relations, and crisis management, in particular.

The social media policy document is not a replacement for knowledge. In other words, employees responsible for posting content on social media should already be skilled in social media etiquette and rules. It is certainly not a role for inexperienced interns. They are the people in charge of the public appearance of the company and therefore must have a strong sense of the company's personality, tone, position on important issues, how to engage with other users, how to respond to criticism, and be aware of the future direction of the company.

Additionally, while it is important that the CEO of a small business owns the social media accounts—a surprising number of companies allow employees to set up, and therefore own the company's social media profiles—other employees should be encouraged and incentivised to work together to create and schedule content in alignment with the social media policy document.

One final thing to note before we dive into two vital parts of your social media activity is that your policy document is not a set-and-forget kind of deal. You'll return to it periodically to update and amend various parts as you gain more experience and to keep up with advances in technology.

Attracting Comments, Likes, and Shares – Engaging with Other Users

Never have the mindset that you are bombarding social media users with your posts, whether they be brand-, influencer- or customer-focussed in nature. Remember that these individuals and businesses have chosen to follow you and want to read what you have to say. Do keep in mind, however, that your followers will be accustomed to your unique style of content publishing and any deviation from this may upset your followers. This being said, if you want to engage with your followers, there are a number of ways you can do so without losing them.

Asking questions is a simple way to initiate discussion and draw comments from your followers. Not only will it provide you with valuable audience engagement on your profile but it also gives you an idea of the overall sentiment towards your brand. Coming out and stating directly that you want users to perform an action or get in touch with you is actually very effective in attracting comments, likes, and shares.

Some social media platforms like Facebook, Google+, LinkedIn allow you to create groups, which are incredibly useful for research. Plus, because many people are eager to join exclusive groups, you generate high levels of interest in your brand. Allow the people in your group to direct where the conversation leads after your initial prompts and join in where appropriate. And when participating, stick to the topic at hand and hold back from promoting your own agenda.

You may have seen posts with the hashtag #AMA. It stands for 'Ask Me Anything'. It is a popular tactic that invites users to ask open and honest questions to develop public trust of a brand or well-known individual. This notion of transparency makes the holder of these AMA sessions more trustworthy and their reputation skyrockets.

AMA sessions for a B2B brand can be used to explain how your brand operates behind the scenes or provide information your followers may not previously have been aware of. As a result, you will begin to develop ongoing relationships with new followers and attract new leads.

For branded AMA sessions, it is most often the most influential person at the company who answers questions. If you're worried about answering potentially damaging questions, invite your audience members to submit their questions to you beforehand but try not to memorise your replies or they will look too rehearsed and salesman-like.

Contests are everywhere on social media. And for good reason. They attract some of the highest rates of engagement in terms of likes, comments, and shares. That means that contests end up in the home feed of many more followers and non-followers than you typical posts.

One way to increase your contest engagement further is to allow users to affect the outcome, by voting for the winner, for instance. The challenging part is making the rules clear before launching freebies and contests. If you're going to use this type of engagement strategy, make sure you develop rules and any terms and conditions that are simple to understand. Too challenging and no-one will want to enter. Additionally, many users worry about their own social reputation by entering contests because their friends will be notified when they enter. Keep this in mind when formulating the design of your contest. You may wish to forego the typical 'Like and Share to Win' contest in favour of the opt-in form. The other advantage of this contest type is that you can collect contact information to generate business later.

Freebies are like contests where everyone's a winner. You ask your followers to perform some action such as sharing your posts or filling out their contact details (or completing a survey, which I'll talk about next) and they receive something free in return. The freebie must be something worth performing the action for. This includes free courses (via email or otherwise), free eBooks, free consultations, etc. Basically, if it's something that helps the businesses you want to partner with increase their profits or business practices, and it will enhance your reputation online, then it works as a giveaway.

Conduct surveys and polls to gather opinions from your followers about your brand and the services you offer. Researching in this manner lets you improve your products and services, with the bonus of engaging with your audience in a meaningful way because it says to your audience that you value their feedback and suggestions. Always remember to thank any user who offers their opinion, good or bad. Surveys can be set up on a number of free survey websites and linked to via social media or create polls directly in your posts.

Emoticons have the power to boost engagement by as much as 33% according to some reports. They believe this is because emoticons make brands appear more human, like someone is actually emotionally involved in the interactions between users and the brand. Your brand has a personality, in other words. Post a smiley emoticon and the social media world smiles with you. Use emoticons sparingly, however, and never at a time where their meaning could be ambiguous. And keeping with the personality theme, it can be a good idea to use your first name or that of your social media manager when responding to your followers. Again, it shows that there is a human being behind your brand, not just a cold organisation.

All of the above was written with you as the owner of the page or profile in mind and other users as the ones engaging with your content. You must remember, however, that you are also a user like everyone else and should make an effort to comment on others' posts, share others' posts, and participate in conversations initiated by other users. And whether it happens on your posts or during conversations on others' posts, aim to have a policy in place for responding to any and all comments, both praise and criticism.

How to Uphold a Positive Reputation When Facing Negativity – Responding to Comments & Criticism

If a user says something negative about your brand,

services or employees then you or your social media manager must respond as soon as possible and use it as an opportunity to respond publicly in a way that upholds a positive reputation of your brand.

Ignoring comments or waiting too long to respond is like saying you don't care and that user—and maybe others that note the lack of response—will likely never comment again, or worse, never return to your page and spread negativity via word of mouth.

Similarly, responding quickly but using anything other than positive and grateful language can damage your reputation. Rude, negative, and indifferent responses indicate to users that you don't care. Your goal on social media is relationship building. That includes client retention and new lead generation, which can only be achieved by maintaining good relationships with everyone who contacts your business.

When responding to direct questions, always use the person's profile name. This has two benefits:
1. The original commenter will be notified of your response and either be happy with the response or get in touch with you for further discussion; and

2. You give the original commenter public recognition that you are genuinely happy to hear from them, meaning you welcome comments from your

followers.

The second part of responding positively means using more than a few words in your response. Give a thorough comment—one you would be happy to receive if you made the original comment—and include an open-ended question at the end. As I mentioned earlier, you want the conversation to continue so that the relationship will continue. If you don't want the conversation to continue on social media, give your contact information so that you can continue the discussion via email or telephone (telephone is better in this case because it shows you care enough to resolve this issue immediately).

In sum:

- Make sure to respond positively to your posts, reviews, and questions.
- If a user leaves a comment, thank them directly and sincerely.
- If a user has a complaint, address it quickly with the aim of turning it into an opportunity to discuss it further.
- Answer questions and offer advice and assistance, including your contact details.

138

CHAPTER SEVEN ACTION STEPS:

❑ Create your company's official social media policy document. Include straightforward guidelines for engaging with your followers and responding to comments and criticism.

CHAPTER EIGHT:
MONITORING AND REPORTING

Finding out that something doesn't work is also the first step toward learning what does work.
- DUNCAN WATTS

CHAPTER CONTENTS

- Resources: Costs and Time
- Meeting with Stakeholders
- Tracking via a Social Media Management Tool
- KPIs

The following sections provide a rundown of the initial costs and time required to execute your ongoing social media activities. One thing to note first, however is that I purposely set social media marketing aside until Chapter 9 to give it its own space for discussing the specific required resources. This means ad budgets will not be included in this section.

How Much Is All This Going to Cost?
Resources: Costs

As far as costs go, you'll only be paying for two things: a social media management individual and a social media management tool. Obviously, I can't tell you how much you'll pay someone to manage your social media profiles— you may be managing it all yourself anyway—and I've already listed the prices of the most popular social media management tools on the market.

After the 30-day free trial period, you're looking at just $10.99 per month if you go for the cheapest—and in my opinion best—option, Hootsuite Pro, if billed annually (total upfront cost $131.88 for 12 months). Going with the other two options, Sprout Social and Sendible, will cost you at least $59 per month for their most basic packages; a major outlay for any business.

You could opt for the free version of Hootsuite and spend zero on your social media activity—more suited to bloggers just starting out on social media—but I advise against this because you will miss out on advanced scheduling features, enhanced analytics report, two separate user accounts, and the intelligent content suggestions tool that recommends shareable content and optimal scheduling times.

Resources: Time

The following approach to social media time management is designed to keep time spent researching, creating, scheduling, sharing, and tracking to a minimum.

Researching content worthy of sharing can be found in many ways. Here are three that can save time spent researching:

1. Scroll through the live Twitter stream on Hootsuite to see what's trending. This will throw up tweets that can be retweeted as well as blog articles linked to within popular tweets.

2. Set up the RSS feed in Hootsuite to monitor content from popular blogs and websites

3. Perform a Google search of relevant keywords and checking the news section.

Engaging content takes time to produce. But with a bank of images and the completed editorial calendar a whole six months' worth of content can be scheduled ahead of time. This initial period of content creation, including new profile banners, will likely take a few weeks.

About 15-20 minutes a day can be earmarked for scheduling content; although more than one day can be scheduled at one time if desired. Since each post will be scheduled one by one and a single post takes around a minute to schedule, it should take 5 minutes to schedule 5 daily posts.

Note: Some social media management tools offer a unique auto-scheduler that can import and schedule posts from Excel spreadsheets such as your editorial calendar. However, I believe it is best to schedule them one by one since this is the only way to guarantee posts will be error-free and scheduled correctly.

Following new profiles and liking new pages every month shouldn't take more than a few minutes because you already have a growing list of influencers (see Chapter 6). Similarly, it only takes a few seconds to copy the username of new influencers you come across into the Excel spreadsheet for following later.

Tracking the performance of each profile against KPIs requires approx. 15 minutes at the start of each month as suggested in the editorial calendar.

Therefore, thanks to the early work put into creating content and filling in the editorial calendar, <u>daily social</u>

<u>media tasks can be completed in under an hour</u> (with an extra 15 minutes for the first business day of each month).

Ongoing social media campaign improvement is made possible by measuring a number of metrics including:

1. How the social media pages and posts are performing based on post engagement such as how often and at what times of the day posts are shared

2. Brand engagement such as new followers and mentions of the brand. Monitoring and reporting can be performed on the company's preferred social media management tool.

Some social media platforms also provide a number of tools to help marketers evaluate their efforts. Despite the usefulness of these tools for monitoring performance and researching trends, they cannot provide detailed analysis of website behaviour once users have clicked through to the company website from a post on social media.

Thanks to Google Analytics, you can determine the precise number of visitors, where they came from, which pages they visit and how long they browse the site; all in real-time. This information validates the efforts of the entire team and helps to encourage everyone to continue contributing to social media. Of course, you will have to set aside time for analysing—and learning how, if necessary—website metrics from social media visits.

Accelerate Understanding Within Your Company – Meeting with Stakeholders

Before meeting with stakeholders to discuss your social media strategy, it is important to consider the best way to accelerate understanding since many may not previously be aware of the usefulness of many social media practices, platforms, and tools to your business. Given the low cost of entry, however, your stakeholders will likely be eager to attempt any proposed social media tactic.

If you've never used social media for your business before, you obviously won't be to analyse past performance reports and therefore provide reasonable estimates of expected outcomes for your social media efforts. As a result, no realistic outcomes can be presented to your stakeholders. In this scenario, it is imperative that your stakeholders understand that social media as a lead generation tool is an ongoing learning experience, with intangible results such as increased brand awareness and research opportunities.

If you currently have branded social media profiles, you can support your presentation with strong reasoning based on analysis of past performance—accompanied by a summary of the activities and expected outcomes—for selling your plan and ideas to stakeholders and other decision makers.

Ensure all stakeholders are aware of all important facets

of the strategy including the amount of resources required and how performance will be reported by the end of the meeting.

Tracking via a Social Media Management Tool

Tracking your performance allows you to develop your social media campaign on a continual basis. And reporting your results to stakeholders not only keeps everyone in the loop but presents opportunities for stakeholders to offer suggestions for strategy improvement. Your social media management tool will provide a number of built-in analytics tools to track success on your chosen social media platforms including engagement levels on a branded page and individual post basis.

Some may argue that sites such as Facebook, Twitter, and Google+ already offer in-depth analytics but because they are platform-specific, they force you to login and analyse performance one by one. Additionally, some platforms like Instagram do not currently have this feature.

KPIs – A Waste of Time?

While some social media commentators advise marketers to focus on users' attitude of the brand and observe who is sharing branded content on social media, others argue that social signals such as how many users follow the brand and share content provide a more measurable indication of success; especially at first.

If you are limited by resources in time and budget, tracking engagement in the form of retweets, favourites, comments, likes, shares, and +1s should not be part of the KPIs; particularly for the initial campaign period. Tracking such engagement would require investment into an out-and-out social media analytics tool or upgrading your social media management tool plan, in addition to time spent creating and analysing reports. So you can delve into this enhanced tracking strategy but I would wait until you have established a strong social presence and can therefore justify an increase in resources.

Therefore, the success of your new social media campaign will come in the form of new followers and increased referrals to your company website from social media starting from the first date of your campaign and steadily increasing from that date. Performance should be tracked on your Excel spreadsheet on the first business day of each month and should take approximately 15 minutes to complete.

The following table is an example of a KPI tracking sheet including the current status of Facebook, Twitter, Instagram, Google+, and website links, and outlines the monthly and final (after six months) targets for each platform.

KPIs	Facebook	Twitter	Instagram	Google+	Clicks
Current Status	Page Likes	Followers			Average Clicks
Average Stats	2,537 page likes	5 followers	10 followers	9 followers	
Monthly Target	28 page likes	2 followers per month	10 followers per month	1 follower per month	2 link clicks per post
Final Target	Gain 40 page likes	Gain 10 followers	Gain 16 followers	Gain 5 followers	Increase by 3 per post
Tracking	3,000 page likes	125 followers	200 followers	70 followers	20 clicks per post
	First business day of each month				

Exhibit 8.1   Social Media Strategy KPIs Example

CHAPTER EIGHT ACTION STEPS:

- ❑ Decide on a salary for a social media specialist and a social media management tool based on your budget. These are your total costs.

- ❑ Devise a daily time management plan for your social media activity. Obviously, the more time you can spend on social media, the better your results will be.

- ❑ Plan your meeting with relevant stakeholders. Ensure you present justification behind your strategy and budget to accelerate understanding.

- ❑ Make a table of measurable and achievable KPIs. Determine when you are likely to achieve these results and how you will inform stakeholders.

- ❑ Familiarise yourself with analytics and reporting methods provided by your chosen social media management tool. Run test reports with your stakeholders to optimise the process before the first real report is implemented.

CHAPTER NINE:
SOCIAL MEDIA MARKETING

You need to play to win. But you also have to win to play.

- MICHAEL SCOTT

CHAPTER CONTENTS

- Social Media Marketing
- Sponsored Updates
- Facebook Ads & Boosting Posts
- Promoted Tweets & Promoted Accounts

Allocating little more than employee time and energy into organic social media posts can equate to pretty impressive returns on investment. But an impressive level of success (in relation to your target objectives) can only happen if you're able to capture the attention of your target audience and inspire them to get in touch with you.

Boosting your brand's online awareness and lead generation, in other words, means reaching the right people at the right time. If you're finding it tough to reach enough people in your target audience with your posts, you may decide to give your profiles a shot in the arm through social media marketing.

Not all social media platforms provide support for paid posts, though. LinkedIn, Facebook, and Twitter offer businesses the greatest potential to increase post reach significantly. Post reach in the social media marketing sense can mean both dedicated paid-for posts as well as organic posts backed by a set budget to appear in front of more followers and non-followers.

Spending Money to Make... Likes? – Sponsored Updates

Sponsored Updates are not exactly self-explanatory. You post an update about your company but it doesn't get sponsored by another company or vice versa. Rather, you turn your usual company update that's seen by a percentage of your followers into a advertisement-style company update that's seen by a higher percentage of your followers as well as some non-followers. Why non-followers? Well, you can set the exact audience you wish to target when creating sponsored updates, seeking out the right people and reaching them with exclusive and group-specific content.

Sponsored updates are visible in users' home feed and are denoted with the word 'Sponsored' below the profile name of the individual or brand behind the post.

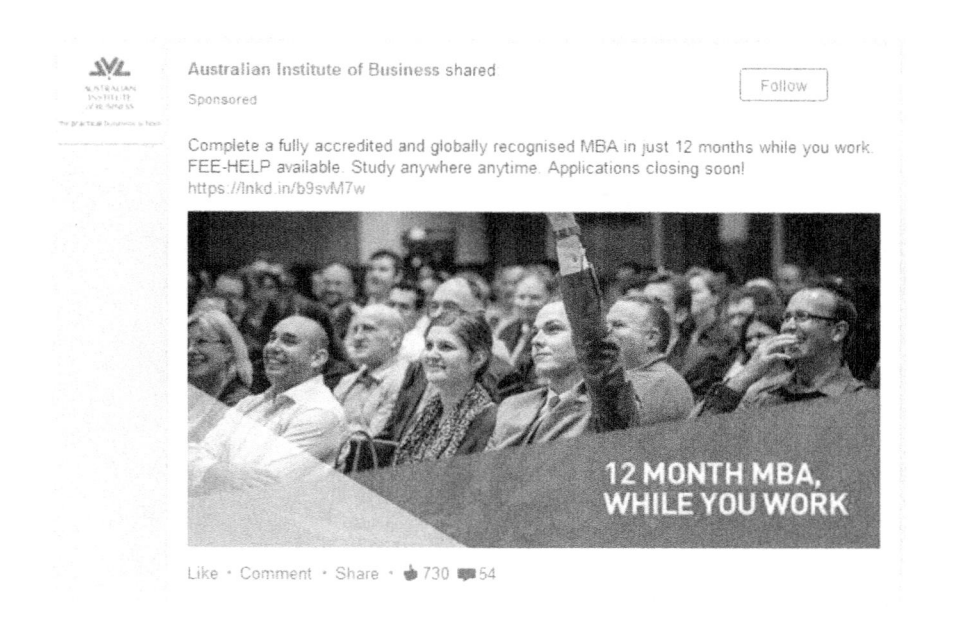

Exhibit 9.1   Ad-Style Sponsored Update

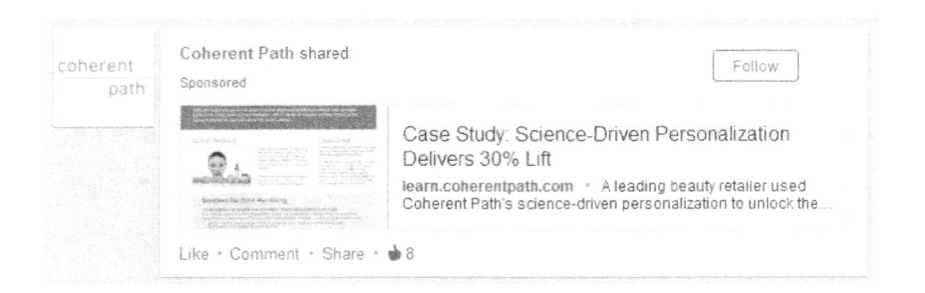

Exhibit 9.2   Article-Style Sponsored Update

Sponsored updates gives you the opportunity to appear within popular and trending content posted by LinkedIn influencers; within the home feed of only those users with qualities and interests you specify.

Additionally, your posts' reach is multiplied wherever users prefer to consume their LinkedIn updates from desktop and laptop to tablet and smartphone. As a result, you can begin to generate truly qualified leads across all platforms.

Why Facebook Ads & Boosting Posts Are Worth It

Facebook ads allow you to place custom content or advert that target a specific audience, with costs increasing depending on the reach and engagement the ad is estimated to receive.

Facebook ads appear in the home feed of your target audience when using both in-home and mobile devices. And if they are using a desktop or laptop computer, your target audience may also see ads in the right column of

Facebook. The ads on the right sidebar appear under the heading SPONSORED rather than the other information you see there including SUGGESTED PAGES and SUGGESTED GROUPS, which are populated based on your personal connections and interests.

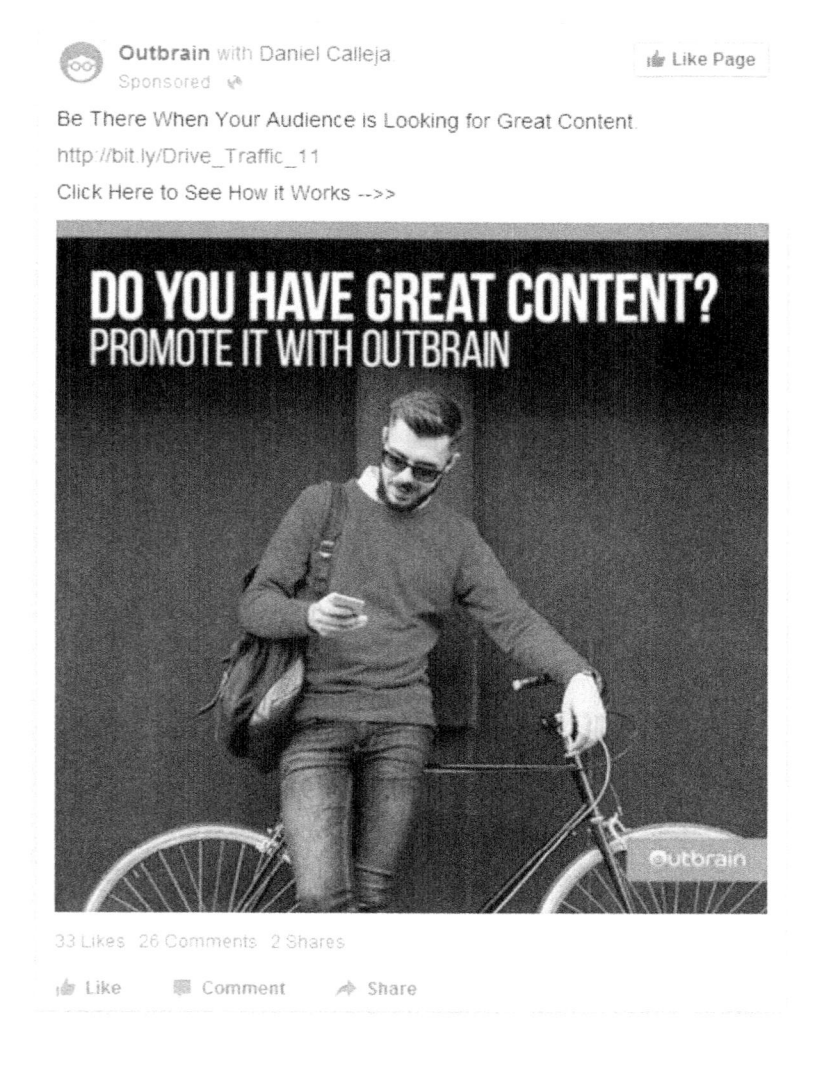

Exhibit 9.3   Facebook Ad in Home Feed

Sponsored

Nike Footwear - Up to 25...
ozsale.com.au
High-quality Nike athletic
footwear for active lifestyles

Exhibit 9.4   Facebook Ad in Sidebar

Facebook ads are great for attracting link clicks and drive lots of new traffic to your company website. Ads linking to blog posts are particularly effective for achieving this aim. Unique landing pages are also a good idea to link to because they ensure you build targeted leads rather than allow site visitors to simply leave your site after they read a blog post.

In fact, apart from testing different ad copy and ad images, you'll want to test different landing pages to see which ones convert best and use it in other ad campaigns going forward. This doesn't mean creating totally different pages altogether, though. Change some headings, change an image or two and retest until you get it right. Same for ads.

As far as Facebook ad audience targeting is concerned, it

may be most beneficial to narrow your target as much as possible to get the best ROI possible. Targeting broader audiences may increase your reach but if you're reaching many of the wrong people, you're just throwing away your marketing budget. On the other hand, you don't want your audience to be so small that you spend a lot of money to show your ad to just a handful of uber-targeted leads—unless of course every single lead is worth a lot of money to your business.

The location of your ads is important. For the most part, you will place your ads in the middle feed. Reaching non-fans, however, may mean showing your ads in the right sidebar. This avoids angering Facebook users when they ask themselves, "Who is this company and why are they appearing in my feed?!"

Boosted Posts are slightly different from ads but retain many of the targeting features. When you publish a post on Facebook, you'll see the option to 'Boost' it. This means making sure the post gets seen by more of your followers and friends of followers than would otherwise normally see it. Facebook's algorithms are so sophisticated that a number of factors determine who sees your organic posts. The only way around this—apart from being so unbelievably popular—is to pay to have your post reach more people.

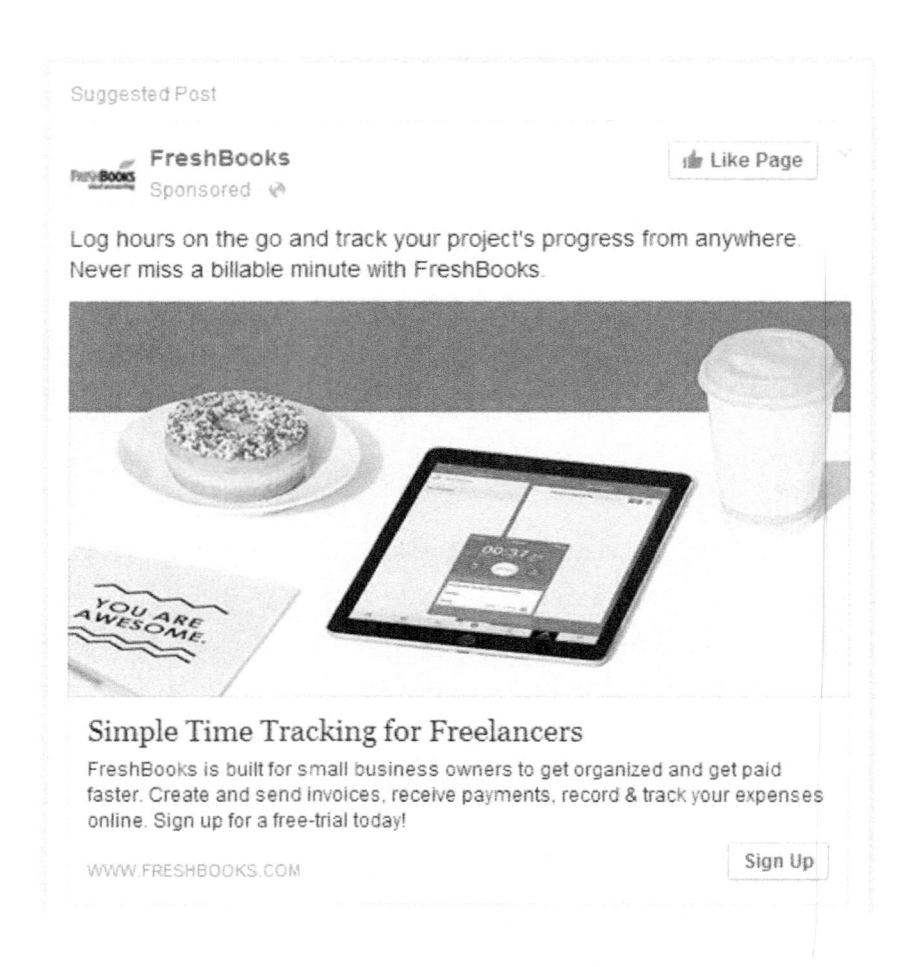

Exhibit 9.5   Facebook Boosted Post

Users see boosted posts the same way they see normal posts; in their home feed. Boosted posts appear higher in users' news feeds, making it more likely your audience will see them. Like Facebook ads, boosted posts are labelled with the word 'Sponsored' and there is no option to make them appear in the right sidebar.

Status updates, photos, videos, and offers are all great

content to boost. Typically, boosted posts are used for the aforementioned content types rather than link clicks. In other words, boosted posts are ideal for building brand awareness rather than increasing site visitors and generating leads. So if your organic posts are not reaching the levels of engagement you were hoping for, by all means boost it. Just remember to track your post performance and use the boost option sparingly. No-one likes to feel that they are being sold to.

Don't Do Promoted Tweets & Promoted Accounts Until You Read This

Promoted Tweets are basically the exact same everyday tweet you see in the live Twitter feed except that they are backed by advertisers. This means they will be labelled with the word 'Promoted' and yet other Twitters can still engage with the promoted tweet like a regular tweet and favourite, comment, and retweet.

If Twitter deems a promoted tweet relevant and interesting to a user, it will appear just once somewhere amongst the top tweets of a user's timeline and also in the results when a user performs a keyword search.

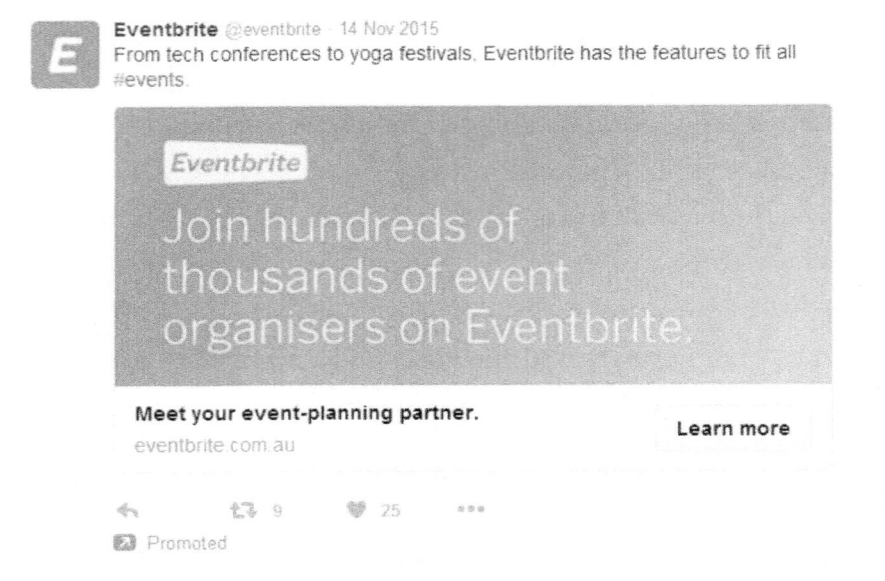

Eventbrite @eventbrite · 14 Nov 2015
From tech conferences to yoga festivals, Eventbrite has the features to fit all #events.

Meet your event-planning partner.
eventbrite.com.au

Learn more

↩   🔁 9   🤍 25   •••

🔗 Promoted

Exhibit 9.6   Promoted Tweet

With similar reasoning behind sponsored updates on LinkedIn and Facebook ads or boosted posts, you want to promote only your best tweets to ensure that: 1.) you build brand awareness; and 2.) you don't annoy users with constant marketing efforts.

Winning with promoted tweets involves enticing a greater audience to perform a certain action such as clicking on a link to your landing page or contact form, signing up for an email newsletter, or claiming a freebie or new promotion. And with greater tweet reach, there's more of a chance that your tweet will appear in the feed of an influencer who will retweet it and give a further awareness boost.

Promoted Accounts, as the name suggests, means promoting your account so that it shows up in the list of suggested accounts for Twitter users to follow.

Promoted accounts appear in various places on Twitter, depending on the page the user is on at that moment. For instance, your profile could be displayed in the list titled 'Who to Follow' or in the results of a Twitter search or even in a user's live feed.

Like promoted tweets, promoted accounts are labelled with the word 'Promoted' for users to tell the difference between the usual recommended accounts and those of advertisers that may be relevant and interesting to them.

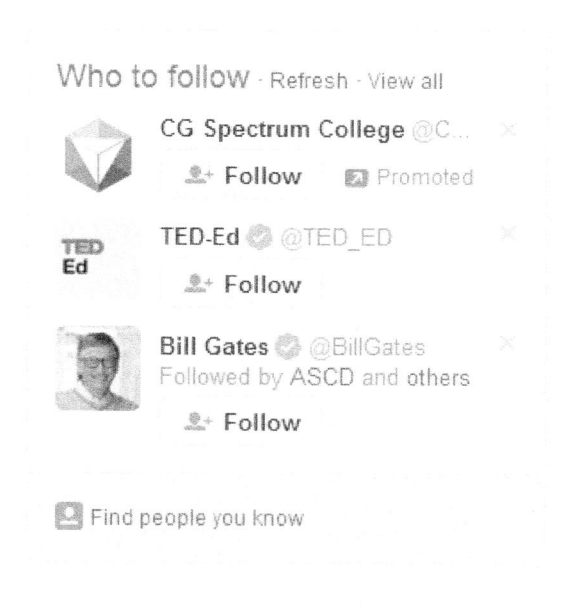

Exhibit 9.7   Promoted Account

In a space where popularity rules, having a ton of followers is a sign of your authority. It says to other Twitter users that you are someone worth following. And since your tweets end up in the live feed of your followers, you significantly increase the reach of your brand messages.

CHAPTER NINE ACTION STEPS:

❏ Familiarise yourself with the paid-for options within LinkedIn, Facebook, and Twitter—not to start posting ads but more to answer any questions you may have and understand any features not covered in this chapter.

❏ If you plan to use social media marketing, add budgets for each platform in your list of costs as well as targets for ROI.

PART IV

A Case Study

This section takes everything I've talked about so far in this book and shows how I applied this knowledge to assist a small ad agency develop their effective yet resource-lite social media strategy.

Part I of this case study will explain my reasoning behind selecting certain social media platforms and rejecting others, which social media management tool I chose and why (I left a hint earlier in the book so you have guessed it already), and the types of content I advocated based on the agency's target audience.

Part II of this case study presents my completed social media cheat sheet and detailed editorial calendar. If the agency ever need to train a new employee to manage their social media, the editorial calendar will be supported by their branding standards to ensure a consistent content style and tone.

For the final part of the case study, I wanted to bring the entire strategy together and show you exactly how the ad agency will perform their daily social media activity on a typical day, which I hope will hit home as to how straightforward and resource-friendly your strategy can be.

Chapter 12 summarises the previous 11 before discussing possible paths for future growth on social media and further boosting lead generation. I've also combined all the action steps from Chapters 1 through 9 into one complete checklist that you and/or your team can use to start profiting from social media.

CHAPTER TEN:
AD AGENCY ON SOCIAL MEDIA
PART I

Never stop testing, and your advertising will never stop improving.

- DAVID OGILVY

CHAPTER CONTENTS

- Platform Selection
- Social Media Management
- Target Audience Interests
- Types of Content

Who They Are and Where They Should Live Online

Founded in 2013, the ad agency Sagada (a pseudonym) is a relative newcomer to the advertising industry, specialising in developing branding and design for local and national businesses, non-profit organisations, and governmental departments. Sagada's personality permeates the agency from its unique monochrome branding through to the stylish office décor; and even dictates the agency's behaviour. Sagada's personality is exemplified on their website and across their current social media profiles on Twitter and Facebook.

Sagada faces a number of challenges in their highly-competitive local area, namely:

- Ranking on page one of Google Search results and being listed on Google Maps for relevant keywords such as "ad agency [city]" and "marketing agency [city]".

- Generating interest from new prospects over and above referrals from former and existing clients.

- An employee roster of just three people: the CEO, the lead designer, and a website programmer.

And with 10 other local advertising agencies offering the same core services, plus additional services that Sagada do not offer, Sagada could be at a disadvantage when trying to attract new clients. To overcome these difficulties, Sagada must demonstrate their unique cultural difference on social media and emphasise their specialist skills in branding and design.

Therefore, the following three objectives provided underlying support to the Sagada social media strategy:

1. Use social media tools to increase social media presence and boost brand awareness online.

2. Use social media tools to build stronger relationships with existing clients and develop new business connections.

3. Engage in two-way interaction with clients, customers and other professionals within the advertising, marketing and branding industries.

The success of the strategy will come in the form of new likes, new followers, new conversations, and increased conversions on the Sagada website directly linked to referrals from social media starting from the first date of the campaign and steadily increasing from that date.

Considering social media selection for ad agencies in particular, the most natural choices for Sagada were LinkedIn, SlideShare, Twitter, Google+, and Pinterest. As the most powerful lead generation tool for B2B companies,

LinkedIn was chosen as the main focus of the social media strategy for Sagada. Additionally, the ability to provide measurable results and repurpose content shared on LinkedIn, Sagada is well positioned to become an authority among the SlideShare community and attract more visitors to their website.

Despite a short history, Sagada has already established itself as an ad agency capable of working with exciting brands on innovative campaigns. Therefore, Twitter provides an excellent opportunity for Sagada to capitalise on its partnerships and reach a larger audience.

Based on the potential to increase search rankings, Sagada stands to gain significant brand awareness from using Google+ as a platform for sharing updates with other users. Additionally, it is unlikely that Sagada will be considered a spam account, aiming instead to showcase their skills in creative design and often educate other users in best branding practices, which is why Pinterest was added to their social media strategy.

The type of clientele that Sagada wants to attract are less likely to use Facebook for discovering business opportunities, and for that reason Facebook was not included in Sagada's social media campaign. Moreover, the abovementioned three reasons, short post life, no backlink support, and a younger demographic, makes Instagram a less appealing medium for ad agencies and was also not included in the Sagada social media strategy.

YouTube was not chosen as part of the social media strategy for Sagada simply because they did not have the resources to create and upload video content. As a Google service that ingrates effortlessly with Google+, however, it will remain on the radar until the company is in a position to create videos on a regular basis.

Step one for Sagada was to update the company profile section across all social media accounts using branded text and images in addition to embedding website links. Based on the recommendations on completing a professional business profile outlined in Chapter 3, the following sections describe the action taken to update Sagada's social media profiles.

LinkedIn

The Sagada LinkedIn profile was already live before I began working with Sagada and included optimised text and links to the Sagada website. However, as I described in Chapter 3, one of the ways to build a larger, more targeted following on LinkedIn is via Showcase Pages; dedicated business pages primarily used to highlight initiatives of various business units within an organisation.

This, then, allows LinkedIn users to follow those sections of Sagada's business with which they have a specific interest in. A quick search of local advertising agencies revealed that not many are taking advantage of Showcase pages, which presents an opportunity for Sagada to dominate this space. The addition of extra pages may give the impression of extra work for the social media manager but posts to the main company page and the six Showcase pages for each business unit will be published on a rotating basis.

SlideShare

A new SlideShare account was opened to ensure the desired username was not acquired by another user. Since no content had ever been created for SlideShare, it wasn't yet necessary to upload and update Sagada's SlideShare profile information.

Twitter

The Sagada Twitter profile was updated with their brand tagline as well as an enticing call to action, "Talk to us about building your business". The full length of the bio was 136 characters including spaces. The location was also updated.

Sagada's Twitter posts will respect the brand persona and adhere to the schedule dictated in the editorial calendar described later.

Google+

Updating Sagada's Google+ account presented a number of challenges because opening a Google+ business page requires a user to first open a Google+ personal page. This allows the personal user to manage any and all business pages from a single account; a similar requirement of Facebook.

However, there already existed a Sagada personal page, which acted as the business page for Sagada, and could not be transferred into a business page. On the surface this may not appear to be an issue but when verifying business information in order to display the business location, hours, and contact details on Google Search and Google Maps results, a Google+ business account is essential.

To overcome this issue, the existing Sagada Google+ personal page was edited to reflect a personal account, including adding a profile image of an individual from a stock photo website, changing the city location to Australia, and deleting all previous posts about the business.

At the same time, a new Sagada Google+ business page was set up and verified with the business details, in addition to profile text, business updates, images, and videos previously published on the personal page.

The next challenge came by surprise when the incorrect contact telephone number appeared after searching for Sagada on Google. A search of the correct number on Google revealed that a business in a different Australian city had verified this number on their Google+ business account. A Google support representative was able to resolve the issue via telephone after it was discovered that the other business had ceased operations and no longer required their Google+ page. I include this information for your reference in case you come across the same situation.

To ascertain whether a regularly updated Google+ profile affects search rankings, an initial snapshot of current results was taken. Of the top five businesses in a search of the keyword "ad agency", not a single one had a complete or regularly updated Google+ business page. This may present a valuable opportunity to increase search rankings and perhaps the chance to rank in position one for Sagada's local area.

Pinterest

Pinterest is the ideal platform to showcase the magazine-quality design work created by Sagada to like-minded designers. As content is created, new boards will be added for displaying high-resolution vertical images from in-house campaigns, campaigns from other agencies, inspirational images, brand persona-related quotes and designs, and the behind-the-scenes work culture at Sagada. The initial profile bio text included a design-related quote that aligns with Sagada's company values. This quote is scheduled to be updated once a month to generate more interest in Sagada's Pinterest account.

New Pinterest boards will make use of keywords

relevant to Sagada's services; a common technique for optimising search rankings. The content strategy for Pinterest will involve repurposing SlideShare presentations as infographics. Infographics, visual representations of information such as statistics, usually have a tall portrait orientation, which consumes valuable real estate on Pinterest's search pages.

After registering for and optimising profile information on the five platforms, LinkedIn, SlideShare, Twitter, Google+, and Pinterest, it was necessary to select a social media management tool to assist the social media associate at Sagada.

But first I must reveal that the situation I found myself in at Sagada was a unique one. In addition to running the company and all sales and marketing efforts, the CEO would also manage social media activity. Yet despite dealing with five diverse social media platforms, the following sections outline how I developed an easily-executable strategy thanks to Hootsuite and an editorial calendar; saving time and effort in any way I could, without letting goal achievement suffer.

Social Media Management Based on Needs and Budget

All three social media management tools I described in Chapter 6 include a 30-day free trial, a mobile app to perform tasks on the go, location targeting, the ability to auto-schedule posts, assign tasks to other users, calendar view, and permission controls to prevent potentially damaging content being posted by accident.

Upon comparison of the three popular social media management tools, and based on the needs and budget of Sagada as a small business and design-focussed ad agency, the appropriate tool for this strategy was Hootsuite.

Hootsuite supports managing Sagada's profiles on LinkedIn, Twitter, Google+ and Pinterest—and supports Facebook and YouTube if Sagada wish to increase their social media engagement at some point in the future. At the time of writing, Hootsuite does not support SlideShare, which, as stated previously, is a platform that will feature heavily in the Sagada social media strategy. On the plus side, Hootsuite has the best content curation, scheduling, and third-party app integration I've seen. And it's the cheapest!

A new account was set up by the Sagada CEO. A quick Google search for any available discount codes produced one result, which provided a further 20% off the Pro annual plan in addition to saving 30% compared to paying $15.99 month by month. Exhibit 10.1 is a screenshot of the stream-style layout and navigation on the home screen of a Hootsuite Pro account.

To monitor performance and improve social media

efforts, the Hootsuite dashboard was optimised to generate reports for Sagada stakeholders. Based on the objectives outlined in their strategy, as well as the time and resources required to manage Sagada's social media accounts, reports

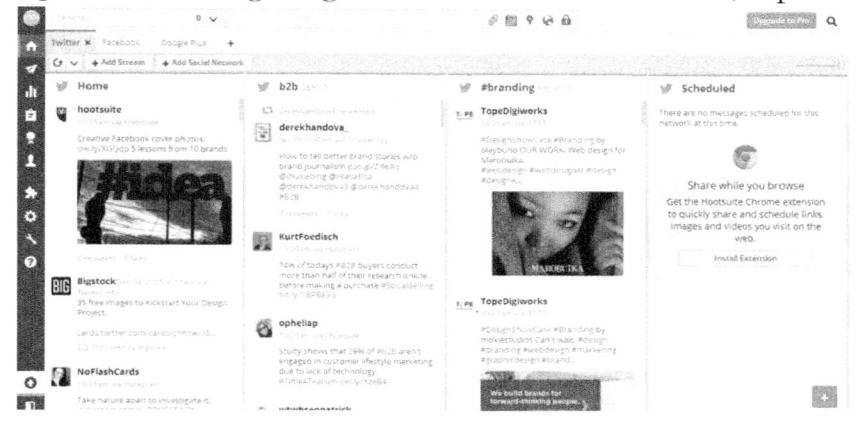

Exhibit 10.1   Hootsuite Twitter Streams

from Hootsuite and Google Analytics were to be generated on the first Monday morning of every month. As a consequence of constant monitoring, their strategy could be quickly changed in response to results.

Target Audience Interests

Sagada's target audience are the decision makers of pretty much any local or national business looking to reach their goals through branding or advertising campaigns. I came to this conclusion after consulting with Sagada's SEO and finding out more about past and current clients. I listed the target audience segments as follows:

- Male Business Managers

- Female Business Managers
- Male Sales and Marketing Professionals
- Female Sales and Marketing Professionals

Why divide them by gender? Well, with the most popular Pinterest content heavily skewed towards women and research findings indicating a male majority on Google+, it made sense to at least figure out their potentially different interests whether I advised Sagada to divide their content strategy or not.

So with the target audience identified as business managers and sales and marketing professionals, I made a table of where they are likely to hang out as well as their interests to help hatch a plan for content.

The table was not purely guesswork, however. I researched what business managers and sales and marketing professionals were engaging with on LinkedIn, Twitter, Pinterest, and Google+; three social media platforms with a strong professional user and business base. In other words,

I made use of the handy streams and free apps on Hootsuite as much as I could to observe the type of content that's being shared and by who, the type of articles that are attracting comments and who is commenting, and trending topics or hashtags. You'll notice I didn't waste a lot of time and energy on creating surveys. I basically wanted to know what these types of people are most interested in and figure out a way to capitalise on this information.

Male Business Managers	Female Business Managers	Male Sales & Mark. Pros	Female Sales & Mark. Pros
LinkedIn, Twitter, Google+	LinkedIn, Facebook, Twitter, Pinterest	LinkedIn, Instagram	Facebook, Twitter, Pinterest
Business growth	Business growth	Design tips & tricks	Design tips & tricks
Business management tools	Business education	Marketing ideas	Marketing ideas
Industry news	Women in business	Branding guides	Inspiring marketing campaigns
Recruitment	Luxury travel	Sports marketing	Digital advertising
Cars and motorcycles	Industry entrepreneurs	Fun advertising campaigns	Fashion and luxury brands

Platforms	Interests

Exhibit 10.2   Interests by Professional and Gender

As I mentioned before, interests across your targeted demographics may vary widely and make it challenging to share content that will engage everyone. Fortunately, I found that Sagada's audience had pretty similar interests.

Cross-referencing the fan interests of each audience segment into a single list suggests that the main content types to target should fall under these five general categories:

- Design tips & tricks
- Branding guides & quotes
- Examples of effective advertising
- Client profiles; especially those with interesting and inspiring owners and staff
- Industry news & Sagada behind the scenes

Now in charge of completed social media profiles and having a good grasp on what their potential clients are interested in, the next item on my checklist was to determine what kind of content Sagada will produce and share.

Types of Content

The question, "What type of content do I want to create?" was answered by uniting the interests of Sagada's audience with the optimal use of each social media platform. It was also necessary to point out that the CEO did not have to create fresh content every week. In fact, it would be impossible given other commitments. Sharing articles and infographics is fine as long as Sagada remembers to always attribute the original source.

The following list shows which types of content are to be created and shared across the five selected platforms:

- LinkedIn
  - Company updates
  - Industry news
  - SlideShare presentations
  - Articles on branding and design

- SlideShare
  - Expert presentations on branding and design

- Twitter
  - Amplify posts on other platforms
  - Retweet influencer content

- Google+
  - Blog articles
  - Educational guides

- o YouTube videos

- Pinterest
  - o Behind-the-scenes company and employee images
  - o Current and past campaign images
  - o Educational infographics
  - o Fun/Inspirational quotes

Answers to the questions, "How often do Sagada want to post on each platform?" and "What days and time should Sagada post?" will be revealed in the next chapter as I describe how I develop Sagada's social media cheat sheet and editorial calendar.

As I hope you remember, the editorial calendar helps streamline the social media strategy and maintain consistency over time by discovering the optimal days and times for posting. Meanwhile, the social media cheat sheet hangs on the wall and provides a quick overview of daily, weekly and monthly tasks for each social media platform, and supports the more detailed editorial calendar. I'll discuss each of these things in Part II of this case study next.

CHAPTER ELEVEN:
AD AGENCY ON SOCIAL MEDIA
PART II

You've got to believe in your work. Only a deep belief will generate the vitality and energy that give life to your work.

- BILL BERNBACH

CHAPTER CONTENTS

- Completed Cheat Sheet
- Completed Editorial Calendar
- Content Style Guide
- A Typical Day: Step-by-Step Walkthrough

This second part of the case study explains how to create an effective social media campaign and outlines how Sagada will design, collect, schedule, and share content on their chosen platforms.

Content should follow the top five audience interests: 1) Design tips & tricks; 2) Branding guides & quotes; 3) Examples of effective advertising; 4) Client profiles; especially those with interesting and inspiring owners and staff; and 5) Industry news & Sagada behind the scenes. And of course aim to feature people in the content where possible.

Content will fall into one of five categories to be posted on specific days of the week. This will make content creation and scheduling more consistent and less time consuming. It also sets the expectations of Sagada's followers. If a follower is interested in Sagada's educational content, then they will become conscious of their routine to post expert tips and tricks every Wednesday.

The five categories as shown in Exhibit 11.1 were colour-coordinated in parallel with the cheat sheet and editorial calendar. For me, having this visual connection between the content types and the day of the week means knowing exactly what kind of content Sagada will create, schedule and share that day at a glance.

Industry	Company	Educate	Entertain	Fun/Quotes
- Industry News - Expert Views - Interviews - Partner Brands - Advertising Legends	- Product Info - Exclusive Brand News - Milestones - The Sagada Culture - Behind the Scenes	- Branding Guides - How-To Presentations - Instructional Videos - Instructional Tips	- Entertaining - Upcoming Events - Festivals - Community Groups	- Fun Adverts - Quotes - Public Figures - Inspirational Campaigns

Exhibit 11.1   Content Types Split into Daily Categories

Completed Cheat Sheet

The one-page cheat sheet was developed before Sagada began its social media campaign. Using the editorial calendar prioritises at what times of day and for how long the CEO will log in to Hootsuite to review brand mentions, reply to messages, and perform any other platform-specific tasks such as following users and sharing others' posts.

Recall that Sagada's social media content creation, scheduling, and monitoring duties will all be performed by the CEO; unless they bring in a talented intern. That meant condensing social media activity into specific times during the working week only and omitting evenings and weekends from the strategy. Further time reduction was necessary to reap the most rewards out of a consistent strategy with the minimal amount of time put in. As a result, daily activity was limited to just 15 minutes per day at around 10am each morning Monday to Friday.

Here's how it looked on the Sagada one-page cheat sheet, which I designed with Sagada's unique branding in mind, using their monochrome tones and particular font style. I'll go further into Sagada's Content Style Guide in a moment after discussing the editorial calendar.

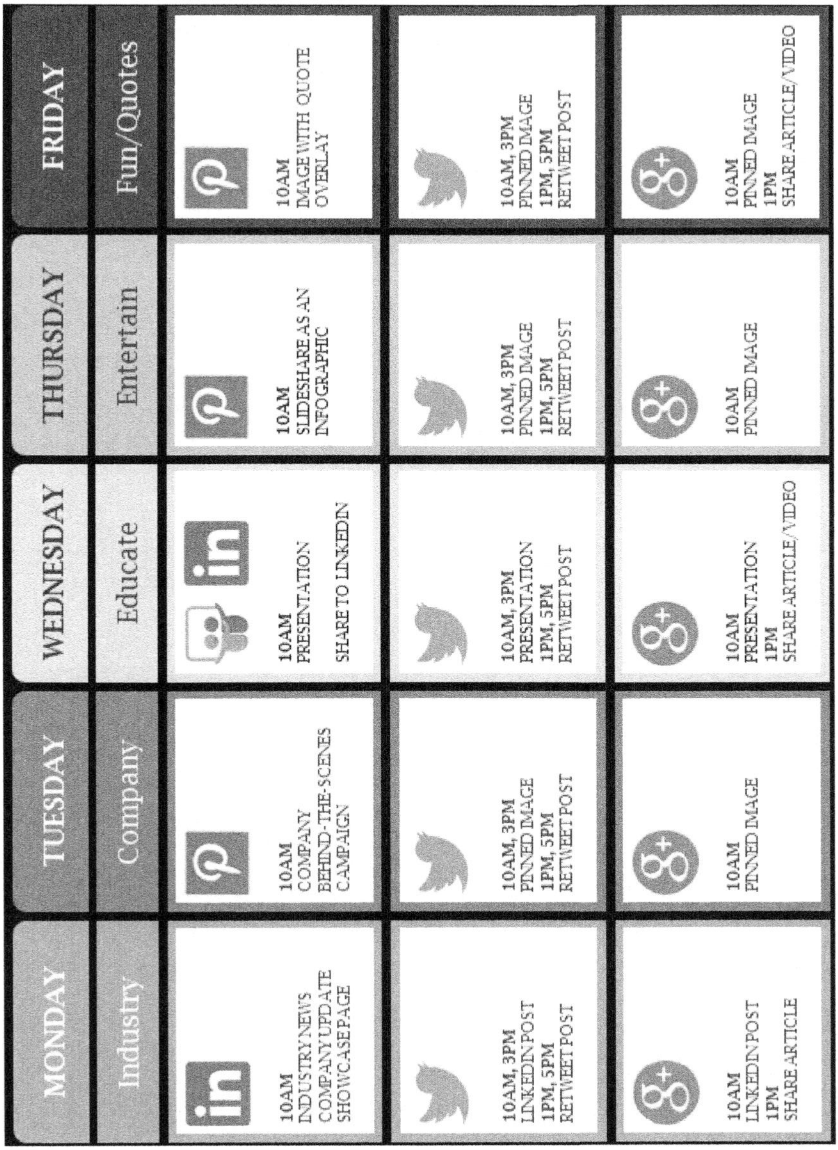

| MONDAY | TUESDAY | WEDNESDAY | THURSDAY | FRIDAY |
Industry	Company	Educate	Entertain	Fun/Quotes
10AM INDUSTRY NEWS COMPANY UPDATE SHOWCASE PAGE	10AM COMPANY BEHIND-THE-SCENES CAMPAIGN	10AM PRESENTATION SHARE TO LINKEDIN	10AM SLIDESHARE AS AN INFOGRAPHIC	10AM IMAGE WITH QUOTE OVERLAY
10AM, 3PM LINKEDIN POST 1PM, 5PM RETWEET POST	10AM, 3PM PINNED IMAGE 1PM, 5PM RETWEET POST	10AM, 3PM PRESENTATION 1PM, 5PM RETWEET POST	10AM, 3PM PINNED IMAGE 1PM, 5PM RETWEET POST	10AM, 3PM PINNED IMAGE 1PM, 5PM RETWEET POST
10AM LINKEDIN POST 1PM SHARE ARTICLE	10AM PINNED IMAGE	10AM PRESENTATION 1PM SHARE ARTICLE/VIDEO	10AM PINNED IMAGE	10AM PINNED IMAGE 1PM SHARE ARTICLE/VIDEO

Image source: Author.

Exhibit 11.2   Sagada One-Page Cheat Sheet

The cheat sheet shown in Exhibit 11.2 will continue to

guide the daily social media activity and participation for Sagada:

- Every Monday at 10am
    - o Post an industry-related news article or announcement, company update or Showcase page article on LinkedIn.
    - o Tweet LinkedIn post and schedule the same tweet for 3pm with alternate text.
    - o Schedule a retweet for 1pm and 5pm.
    - o Share LinkedIn post on Google+.
    - o Schedule an industry-related article on Google+ for 1pm.

- Every Tuesday at 10am
    - o Pin a company-related image (employee profile, behind the scenes or from a campaign).
    - o Tweet pinned image and schedule the same tweet for 3pm with alternate text.
    - o Schedule a retweet for 1pm and 5pm.
    - o Share pinned image on Google+.

- Every Wednesday at 10am
    - o Upload an educational SlideShare presentation or embed a presentation on LinkedIn profile or Showcase page.
    - o Tweet presentation and schedule the same tweet for 3pm with alternate text.
    - o Schedule a retweet for 1pm and 5pm.

- o Share presentation on Google+.
- o Schedule an educational article or YouTube video on Google+ for 1pm.

- Every Thursday at 10am
  - o Pin the SlideShare presentation as a single image or infographic.
  - o Tweet pinned image and schedule the same tweet for 3pm with alternate text.
  - o Schedule a retweet for 1pm and 5pm.
  - o Share pinned image on Google+.

- Every Friday at 10am
  - o Pin fun image or image with quote overlay.
  - o Tweet pinned image and schedule the same tweet for 3pm with alternate text.
  - o Schedule a retweet for 1pm and 5pm.
  - o Share pinned image on Google+.
  - o Schedule a fun article or YouTube video on Google+ for 1pm.

While not contained in the cheat sheet, the Sagada CEO will follow influencers in the advertising and marketing industries and regularly follow other accounts that frequently post engaging, shareable content.

Completed Editorial Calendar
The additional, more detailed editorial calendar was then developed to guide content publishing, following the above

Exhibit 11.3 Sagada Detailed Editorial Calendar

Image source: Author

	A	B	C	D	E	F	G	H	I	J
1	PUBLISH DATE	TIME	PLATFORM	CONTENT TYPE	AUTHOR	DRAFT TEXT	LENGTH	ASSETS & LOCATION	STATUS	RETWEET
2						WEEK 1				
3	04/01/2016	10am	ALL	KPI Tracking					Published	
4	04/01/2016	10am	LinkedIn	Industry news	RW		277	N:\Users\Sagada\Deskt	Published	
5	04/01/2016	10am	Twitter	Linkedin post	RW		92	N:\Users\Sagada\Deskt	Published	
6	04/01/2016	10am	Google+	Linkedin post	RW		184	N:\Users\Sagada\Deskt	Published	
7	04/01/2016	1pm	Google+	Industry article	RW		236	http://www.advertisingv	Published	
8	04/01/2016	3pm	Twitter	Linkedin post	RW		60	N:\Users\Sagada\Deskt	Published	
9	05/01/2016	10am	Pinterest	Recent campaign	RW		61	N:\Users\Sagada\Deskt	Published	
10	05/01/2016	10am	Twitter	Pinned image	RW		100	N:\Users\Sagada\Deskt	Published	
11	05/01/2016	10am	Google+	Pinned image	RW		108	N:\Users\Sagada\Deskt	Published	
12	05/01/2016	3pm	Twitter	Pinned image	RW		77	N:\Users\Sagada\Deskt	Published	Remember
13	06/01/2016	10am	SlideShare	Design guide	RW		461	N:\Users\Sagada\Deskt	Published	retweet as sche
14	06/01/2016	10am	Twitter	Presentation	RW		95	N:\Users\Sagada\Deskt	Published	
15	06/01/2016	10am	Google+	Presentation	RW		113	N:\Users\Sagada\Deskt	Published	
16	06/01/2016	1pm	Google+	How to article	RW		165	http://www.about.com/f	Published	
17	06/01/2016	3pm	Twitter	Presentation	RW		87	N:\Users\Sagada\Deskt	Published	1pm & 5pr
18	07/01/2016	10am	Pinterest	Cool image	RW		93	N:\Users\Sagada\Deskt	Published	
19	07/01/2016	10am	Twitter	Pinned image	RW		101	N:\Users\Sagada\Deskt	Published	
20	07/01/2016	10am	Google+	Pinned image	RW		168	N:\Users\Sagada\Deskt	Published	
21	07/01/2016	3pm	Twitter	Pinned image	RW		86	N:\Users\Sagada\Deskt	Published	
22	08/01/2016	10am	Pinterest	Quote	RW		29	N:\Users\Sagada\Deskt	Published	
23	08/01/2016	10am	Twitter	Pinned image	RW		94	N:\Users\Sagada\Deskt	Published	
24	08/01/2016	10am	Google+	Pinned image	RW		110	N:\Users\Sagada\Deskt	Published	
25	08/01/2016	1pm	Google+	Fun video advert	RW		71	http://youtube.com/rtok	Published	
26	08/01/2016	3pm	Twitter	Pinned image	RW		107	N:\Users\Sagada\Deskt	Published	
27						WEEK 2				
28	11/01/2016	10am	LinkedIn	Industry news	RW		258	htttp://www.moz.com/s	Published	
29	11/01/2016	10am	Twitter	Linkedin post	RW		100	N:\Users\Sagada\Deskt	Published	
30	11/01/2016	10am	Google+	Linkedin post	RW		93	N:\Users\Sagada\Deskt	Published	

I◄ ◄ ► ►I **January 2016** February 2016 March 2016 April 2016 May 2016 June 2016 July

predetermined schedule I made for each platform. I have edited certain areas to protect my client's identity but the calendar in Exhibit 11.3 retains all the important parts.

Content Style Guide

Content published on Sagada's social media platforms had to be consistent in its look and feel. Since social media is a crucial communicative tool for the agency, all content must reflect the Sagada brand, values, and aesthetic. The style guide was established as follows:

- The brand name in all images must use the font Lucida Bright.
- Profile images should have a solid black background with the brand name centred in white text.
- Cover photos should be visually rich and tell a story about the Sagada brand, and include the brand logo in the centre of the image.
- The brand logo will appear on all images across all social media platform unless instructed otherwise.
- Image colours will generally be greyscale, black, and white.
- Always use a friendly tone of voice, with a little bit of humour and cheekiness.
- Keep language succinct and to the point but always define industry terms within educational content.

The Sagada social media strategy was designed to be managed by a single employee via Hootsuite. If the CEO can't continue managing their social media profiles and must hire someone else, an understanding of what makes interesting, shareable text and design is a desirable prerequisite for Sagada's new social media specialist in addition with the commitment to adhering to Sagada's content style guide.

Other employees are encouraged to participate in creating and suggesting content for publishing on social media. And if any user says something negative about the brand, services or employees then the Sagada social media specialist will respond as soon as possible using Hootsuite and use it as an opportunity to respond publicly in a way that upholds a positive reputation of the brand.

A Typical Day: Step-by-Step Walkthrough

I titled this section "A Typical Day". It's probably not the most appropriate title since a typical day requires nothing more than 15 minutes of effort for the Sagada CEO. I'll show you exactly how I advised Sagada spend these 15 minutes every morning.

NOTE: I will use screenshots from my personal digitallyrich accounts to protect my client's privacy. That said, all screenshots will show an identical layout to the one I actually used and will help illustrate my descriptions as much as the original account would.

As explained in Chapter 10, Sagada's social media

profiles were set up on individual tabs within Hootsuite. And within each profile tab are several live streams. For the Twitter account, for example, I added streams for Home, Scheduled, My Tweets, Retweets, and Mentions. Similar, platform-specific streams were also set up for Sagada's LinkedIn and Google+ profiles.

All posting, scheduling, replying, retweeting, liking, content research, and tracking will be performed via these tabs. The following sections explain the Daily Social Media Flow in more detail.

Posting & Scheduling Content

1. To share a message, first choose which social network you would like to share with from the "Send to…" box in the top left corner of the dashboard.

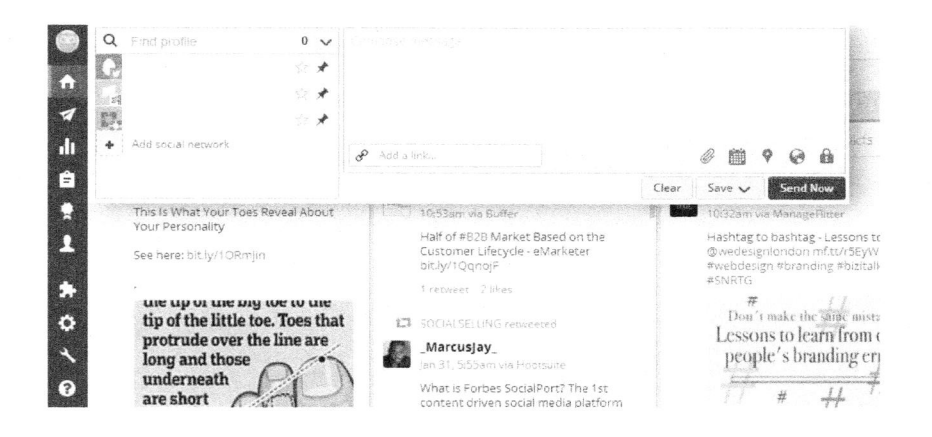

Exhibit 11.4   Composing Messages on Hootsuite

2. Type your message in the Compose Message box.

Paste a URL into the field labelled "Add a link…" and click Shrink (URLs in Facebook and Google+ posts will auto populate with an article summary and thumbnail). Click the Attachment icon to add images (browse folders or drag-and-drop). To **share immediately**, click Send Now.

NOTE: To mention users on Google+ via Hootsuite, use + before the user handle, not @.

Exhibit 11.5   Adding Images on Hootsuite

Exhibit 11.6   Article Summary on Google+ Post

3. Or to **schedule a message for later**, click the calendar icon to view the drop-down calendar. Set the date and time you wish to send your message and hit Schedule.

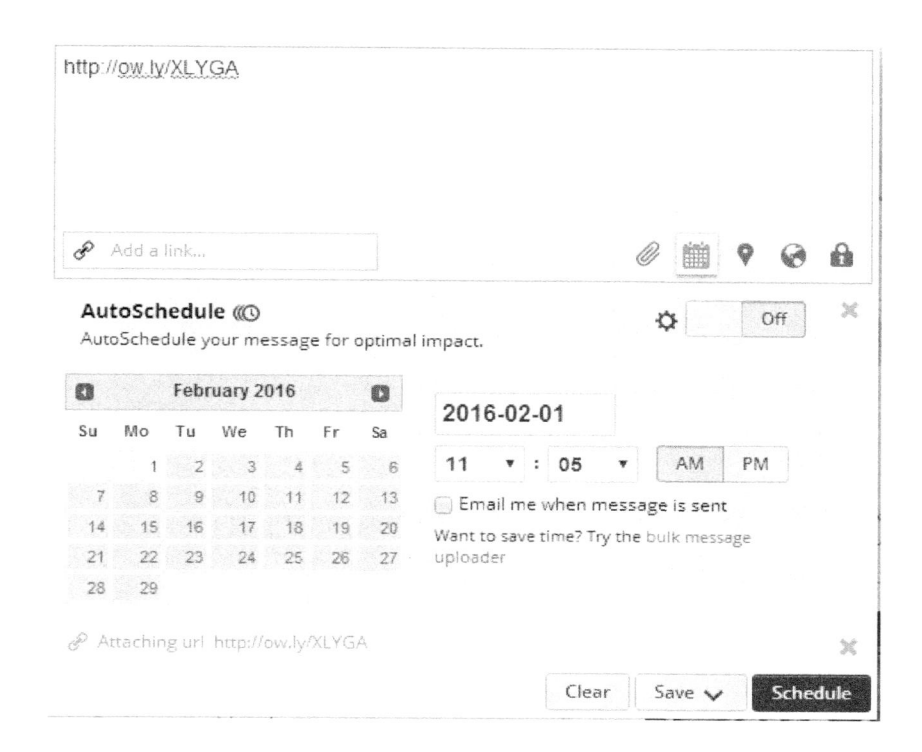

Exhibit 11.7 Scheduling Messages on Hootsuite

4. To **geo-target messages on Twitter**, click on the world icon in the Compose box. Enter a location and language, and click Save or Schedule.

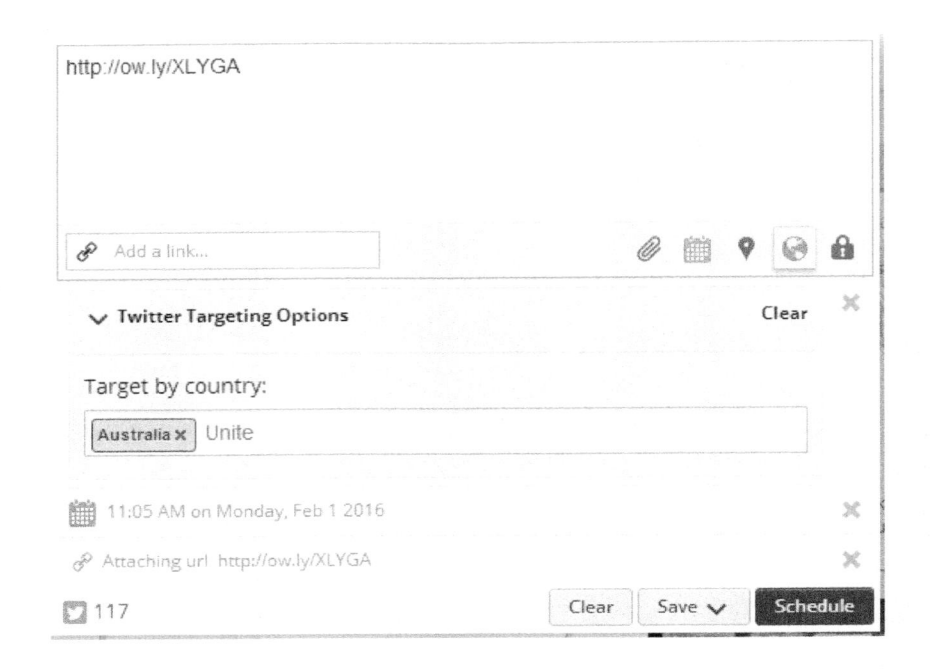

Exhibit 11.8　Geo-Targetting Messages on Hootsuite

Total Time Spent Posting & Scheduling Daily Content = 5 minutes.

Replying, Retweeting & Liking Posts

1. Hover over the post you wish to reply to, retweet or Like to see the interaction icons.

Exhibit 11.9　Interaction Icons on Hootsuite

2. To **Reply,** click the Reply icon. The message box will auto-populate the Twitter username of the post you are replying to. Type your response to the message and click Send.

3. To **Retweet,** click the Retweet icon and then choose one of three options:

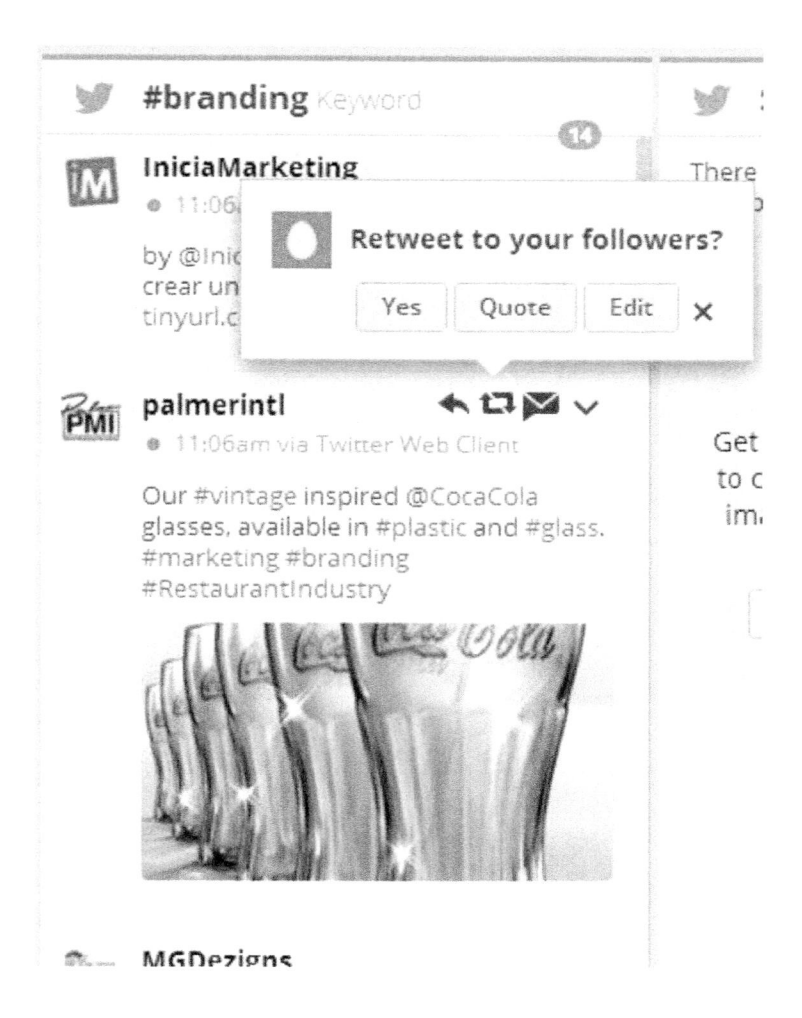

Exhibit 11.10   Retweeting Options on Hootsuite

a. **Yes** – clicking Yes will Retweet the message instantly.

NOTE: This is the only option that will display the text, "Sagada Retweeted" above the tweet.

b. **Quote** – clicking Quote will populate the URL of the tweet in a new message, giving you more space to add your own text. Quote allows you to change the text and schedule the retweet for another time or day. Here's how quotes look on Twitter, with the original tweet on displayed within a box:

Exhibit 11.11   Quote Retweet

c. **Edit** – clicking Edit will populate the Compose Message box with the original tweet preceded by "RT @user:" (to alert the OP) and includes the URL of any attached image. Edit allows you to change the text and schedule the retweet for another time or day.

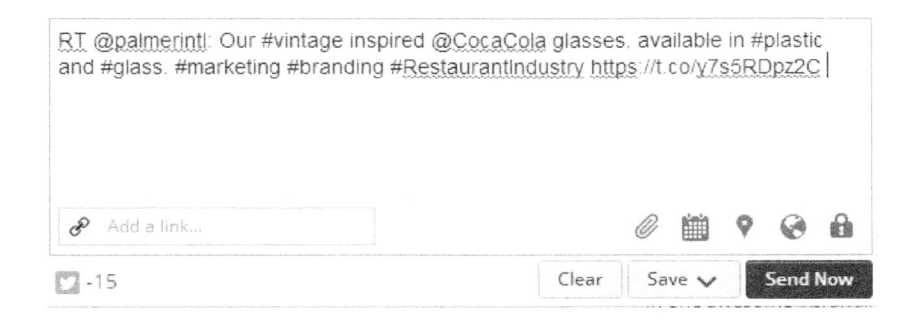

Exhibit 11.12   Editing Retweets on Hootsuite

As I mentioned earlier, editing any tweets with over 100 characters and an image—like the one you can see in Exhibit 11.12—before retweeting will be challenging because adding the Twitter handle or even just "RT" will take it over the character limit. In this case, the retweet is over by 15 characters.

Total Time Spent to Reply to, Retweet & Like Posts = 5 minutes

Research & Curating Content

EXPAND and EXPLAIN Hashtags can be set up on their own streams e.g. if you are attending a conference and want to keep track of the hashtag for the event, you can enter it in the search box and save it as a stream.

The App Directory is a library of free and premium third-party apps you can add to your dashboard. Free apps such as StumbleUpon, Right Relevance, YouTube and Trendspottr are useful for researching content because they help to find trending hashtags and blog posts in addition to monitoring competitor feeds.

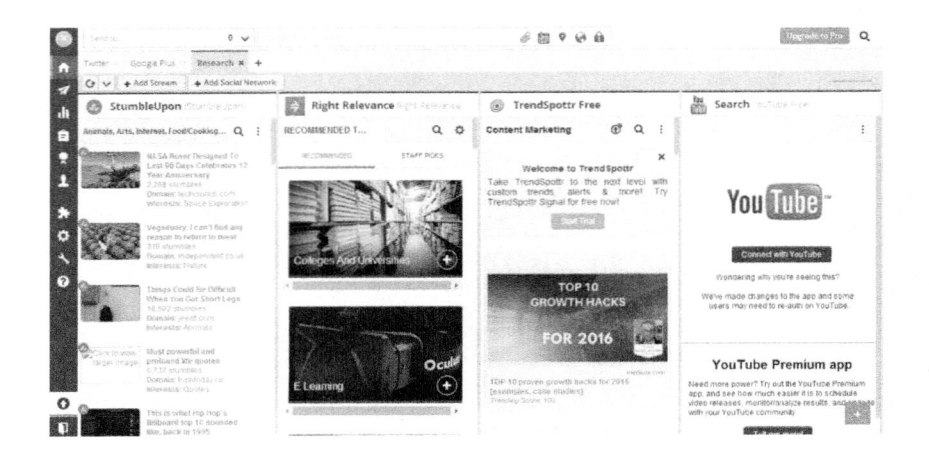

Exhibit 11.13 Apps for Content Research on Hootsuite

Similarly, popular hashtags and influencers can be set up in more than one stream through Hootsuite.

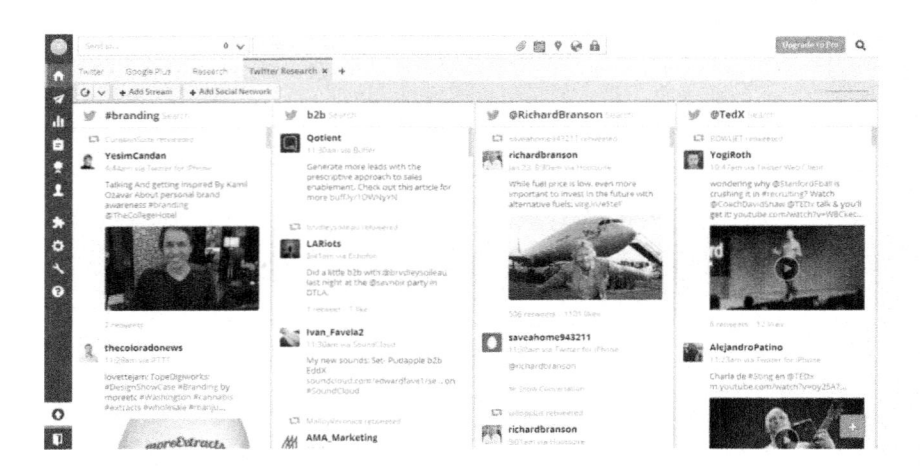

Exhibit 11.14 Streams for Hashtags and Influencers

The advanced Suggestions tool (not available in free plan) in the Publisher section can be used to find relevant articles based on suggestions made by Hootsuite. Articles in this section are easily shared with followers thanks to the automatic text and scheduling settings. Select Edit to change the text or Replace to show a different article suggestion. Click the Settings gear icon to change keywords.

Total Time Spent Research & Curating Content = 5 minutes

Total time spent each day = 15 minutes

Reporting

Ongoing social media campaign improvement is made possible through tracking and reporting. I recommended to Sagada that they create reports for their social media efforts on the first Monday of each month via Hootsuite. Hootsuite provides a number of built-in analytics tools including follower growth, most popular posts, click summary, and popular hashtags.

With Hootsuite Pro you get one customised report per month to track success on Twitter including the total number and detailed analysis of retweets, new followers and mentions.

To create a report:

1. Click the analytics tab in your launch bar and click Build Custom Report.

Exhibit 11.15   Analytics Page on Hootsuite

2. A new browser tab will open. Select a template from the options. Note: some of the options are free but most cost varying amounts of credits. The Pro plan includes 50 credits a month – enough for the Twitter Engagement - Detailed report.

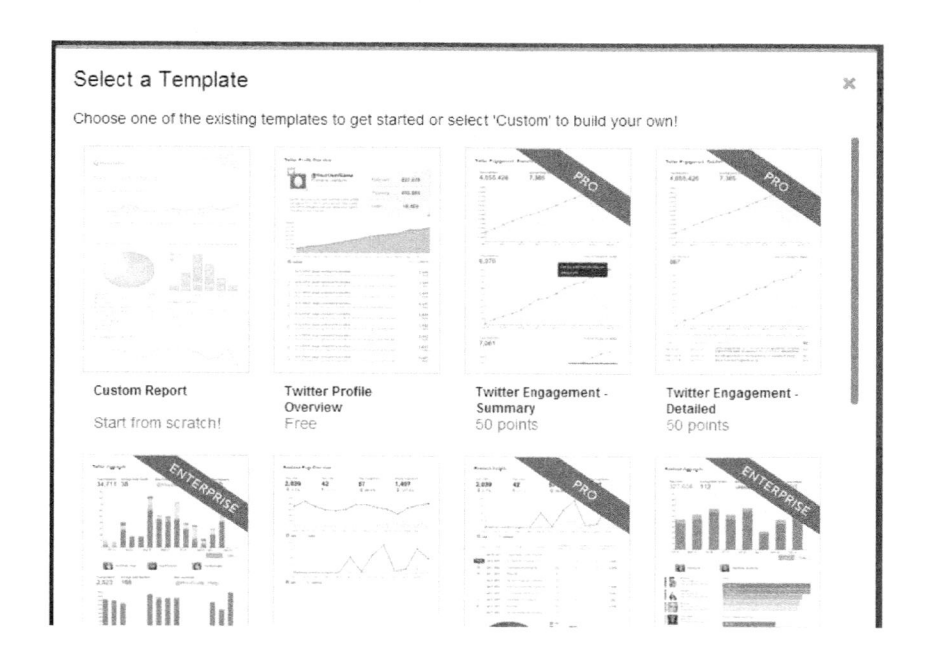

Exhibit 11.16   Report Templates on Hootsuite

3. Select a Twitter profile and then click Continue to Report Builder to see an example of the report. Click Create Report to see the final report.

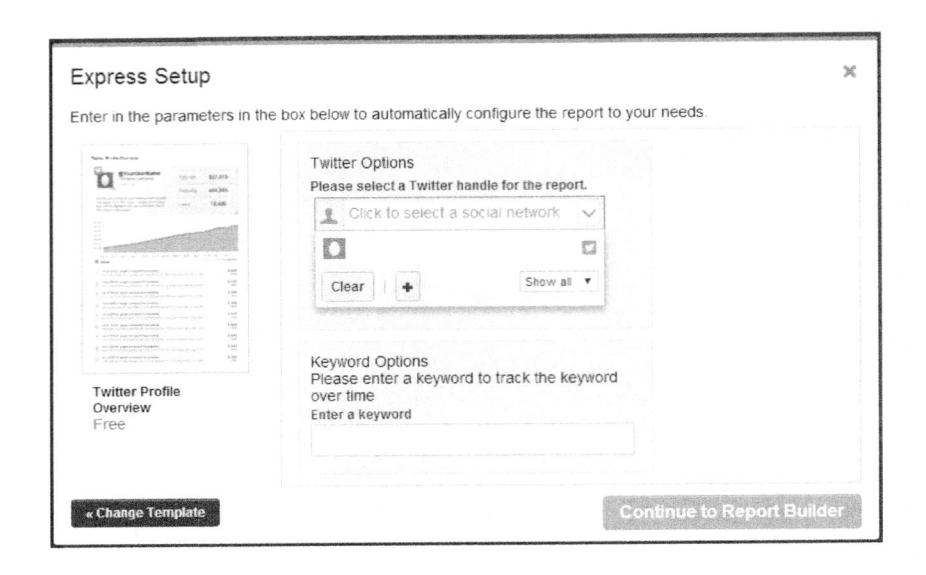

Exhibit 11.17 Report Template Setup on Hootsuite

Hootsuite's Ow.ly URL shortener also allows you to unlock the ability to track link clicks. As your social media profiles grow, more time can be spent examining Hootsuite reports to better understand the impact of your social media activity and track link clicks as part of new KPIs.

Reporting (1st Monday each month) = 15 minutes

Link Tracking

To use link tracking, click the gear icon next to the shrink URL box in the Compose Message box. Select Google Analytics from the Add custom URL parameters drop-down. There are 3 common variables that should always be included:

- Campaign Source (utm_source): Use this to identify

the source of your traffic. Common referrers include social media sites like Twitter or Facebook, a specific newsletter edition, or a site where you have some banner ad placement.

- Campaign Medium (utm_medium): This shows the marketing medium you used your URL in, such as an email newsletter, a specific banner ad size, or CPC.

- Campaign Name (utm_campaign): Create a general theme for your content, and use the same campaign name across mediums and sources to compare results. An example could be "videoinfographic" or "founderscorner3".

In Google Analytics, you can quickly see which URLs with UTM parameters drove traffic by visiting Traffic Sources > Sources > Campaigns. Select the Source / Medium tab in the Primary Dimension section, and then select Campaign as the Secondary Dimension to get an overview of the sources, mediums and campaigns that sent the most traffic.

CHAPTER TWELVE:
TIME FOR ACTION

None of my rules of success will work unless you do.
- ARNOLD SCHWARZENEGGER

CHAPTER CONTENTS

- Summary
- Top Do's & Don'ts
- Future Growth Strategy
- B2B Social Media Checklist

Summary

Thank you for taking this journey with me through strategising your social media plan to developing the tools you'll need to make it a success to putting policies and contingencies in place, and finally, to seeing the entire strategy come together in a real-world scenario. I'd like to go over everything covered up to this point with the aim that reading it all in one place will enhance understanding and reinforce what you learned.

Part I introduced social media for B2B companies. As you'll recall, the most exciting things about social media for B2B is the ease of entry and capacity for generating leads. But the downside to social media for B2B is getting started and keeping things going after you start. This can be tricky for businesses with little resources to devote to tweeting, pinning, and liking.

Thankfully, there are tactics and tools to simplify the entire process. The first of these is defining your objectives for using social media. This will help you select the most suitable platforms for meeting your objectives. The B2B-focussed examination of each of the top eight social media platforms as used by B2B marketers in Chapter 2, then, was meant to be read with objectives in mind.

As I said, knowing more about popular social media platforms is one thing. Knowing how to use them effectively is quite another. Chapter 3 delved into the best practices for each of the top eight platforms, giving you handy tips on content creation and audience engagement. It's also a gateway into your company-specific social media guidelines outlined in Chapter 7.

Chapter 4 was all about content. After pinning down the interests of your audience, it was necessary to begin curating and creating content that aligns with these interests. But that didn't mean erratically posting branded and non-branded content in an attempt to interest your entire audience at once. Instead, it is best to set goals for your content and then create engaging posts according to your own unique set of branding standards. As a result, you will have ongoing effective social media activity and therefore achieve increasing success.

Since consistency is key in any social media strategy—showing up on social media and then vanishing into thin air doesn't sit well with your followers—an editorial calendar will drive your daily social media posts and keep your team aware of what has and what hasn't been scheduled for each platform. The example editorial calendars I presented in Chapter 5 gives you an idea of how your editorial calendar could look as well as how it works alongside a one-page, colour-coded cheat sheet.

Another driving force in maintain consistent engagement with your audience is your social media management tool. Rather than logging in to separate social media platforms and posting content to each, the management tool will significantly reduce the time and effort required to find and schedule content across all of your profiles. And depending in the tool you choose, management through third-party software can be cost-effective.

Part III took a sharp turn away from having fun participating on social media and down a serious path towards managing risk. So while embracing Mr. Zuckerberg's advice to keep up with the ever-changing digital landscape by taking risks, it is important to create a company social media policy document in order to direct appropriate social media behaviour and help prevent a PR disaster. As a result, comments will not go unanswered and enthusiastic interns will avoid inappropriate conversations using your brand's profile.

Sticking with internal contingencies, it is important to keep stakeholders on your side. This is achieved through consistent tracking of your social media ROI and regular reporting to relevant stakeholders. And social media management tools help make this process relatively effortless. Keeping stakeholders in the loop is also vital when it comes to company spending, which was covered in Chapter 9 regarding paid social media posts.

Social media marketing is only available on a few platforms and I covered what kind of ads and sponsored posts you can create on LinkedIn, Facebook, and Twitter.

While I encourage you to strive for high lead generation results with organic posts, it is sometimes necessary to boost your posts with a budget. Situations for paying for greater post reach include seeking new followers for your branded page, broadcasting news about an upcoming event, and making sure your brand sits in user's home feed alongside other industry leaders and authorities in your field of expertise.

The case study in Part IV took everything I discussed in the previous nine chapters of this book and showed you how I applied this knowledge to assist a small ad agency, Sagada, develop their effective yet resource-lite social media strategy.

I hope I competently explained my reasoning behind selecting certain social media platforms and rejecting others, in addition to the social media management tool I chose. The types of content I suggested the brand uses based on the agency's target audience were also given.

Part II of the case study presented my completed social media cheat sheet and detailed editorial calendar. The editorial calendar will assist the agency if they ever need to train a new employee to manage their social media. Plus, their branding standards to ensure a consistent content style and tone. It was my pleasure to work with Sagada and I wish them success in exceeding their social media objectives.

For the final part of the case study, I wanted to bring the entire strategy together and show you exactly how the ad agency will perform their daily social media activity on a typical day, which I hope helped you understand how straightforward and resource-friendly your own social media strategy can be.

Top Do's & Don'ts

Throughout this book I've tried to present best practices for business social media use. To save you flipping through to find them, I've listed the important one to keep in mind here.:

- **Do** invite employees to like company posts.
- **Don't** like your own posts from the company account.

- **Do** follow influencers as scheduled and when appropriate.
- **Don't** follow just anyone or follow lots of profiles at once.

- **Do** respond to all questions & complaints.
- **Don't** simply delete negative comments (unless they contain inappropriate language or content).

- **Do** use relevant, short hashtags.

- **Don't** use hashtags on Facebook, use @mentions instead.

This is by no means a comprehensive list because your social media strategy should be flexible enough to change as social media changes. They should, however, remain relevant to businesses regardless of any future developments.

Future Growth Strategy

After establishing the social media strategy as prescribed in this book, it is beneficial for you to use alternative channels and reach a more diverse audience. This should facilitate more lead generation, and possibly allow you to offer an increased range of services for future clients; taking care to assign more resources to social media incrementally as your business grows.

If more resources become available, it can be a good idea to expand your reach by posting more content and managing new profiles on other social media platforms. With more diverse content at hand, other social networking platforms like Reddit, Flickr, WeChat, etc. can be used to connect with new fans across your region. Fortunately, many of these platforms are supported by popular social media management tools at no additional cost.

If you have the resources, I suggest moving into the world of YouTube. Videos are the most consumed media online and for good reason. The level of engagement you can generate from video content is unparalleled.

As I stated in the Time Zones section, posting at various times in a day and using various content types can engage your fans located in different regions. And if you're running a work-week strategy, you may wish to start posting on weekends. Again, this doesn't mean you or your employees have to work weekends. Simply schedule your posts and retweets to be published during the weekend. You won't be able to respond to any comments at the weekend so keep that in mind when thinking about what you'll publish on Saturdays and Sundays.

Another path you can follow to accomplish accelerated growth involves driving more traffic to your company website and specific landing pages through social media marketing, which as described earlier, ensures your posts are seen by more fans as well as non-fans (depending on your budget and ad objectives).

B2B Social Media Checklist

In this book you have learned what you need to know about developing a social media strategy for your B2B company and benefited from seeing how such a strategy would be developed using a small ad agency as a real life case study. It's now time to go forth and create your strategy. If you haven't been able to perform all the action steps found at the end of each chapter as you reach them, here is the complete B2B social media strategy checklist to make sure you don't leave out any important elements of your strategy.

Tick each item off when complete. A completed checklist means it's full steam ahead.

❑ Get your employees and stakeholders together and as a group agree upon your company's objectives for using social media. Don't worry about coming up with overly detailed objectives at this stage since this is likely your first foray into social media and no past results exist which could help predict comprehensive future objectives.

❑ Include as many measurable objectives as possible as these will better determine if your strategy is working.

❑ Write them down and stick them up on the wall in clear sight of everyone involved in the success of the strategy.

❑ Read an introduction of any of the eight social media sites you're not familiar with before moving on to the next step.

❑ Make a brief list of the advantages and disadvantages of using each of the top eight platforms and how each will help or hinder achieving your objectives.

❑ Go through your list and decide on four social media platforms that you will use in your social media strategy based on your currently available resources.

❑ If you don't have one already, register for an account on each of your chosen platforms using a pseudo personal account and familiarise yourself with the layout, features and typical user behaviour.

❑ Follow some of your competitors and B2B companies in other regions that offer similar services to yours to see how they are using the platform.

❑ If you haven't selected four social media platforms yet, read the best practice guides and determine if you have the required resources to implement them.

❑ If you have selected four social media platforms, make notes of the best practices for future reference when it comes time to create content.

❑ Decide on the username convention for your brand that will be used across all social media platforms.

❑ Update your profiles with brief yet informative bio text, a website link, and consistent branded profile images.

❑ Join communities on LinkedIn, Twitter, Facebook, YouTube, Google+, SlideShare, Pinterest, and

Instagram to find out who your target audience is and what content they like to consume.

❑ Make a table of the five key content types that are gratifying for each audience segment and use this table to make a list of the five key content types that are gratifying across all audience segments.

❑ If applicable, note the different time zones of your audience across your serviced region. Aim to schedule your posts within these time zones to engage everyone.

❑ Make sure everyone involved in the social media content creation and scheduling process understands and follows the rule of thirds. This means posting equal amounts of branded, influencer, and customer content as scheduled in your editorial calendar.

❑ Take a good look at your currently available resources and, based on what you discover, decide on the type of content you want to create.

❑ Decide what you want your content to do; whether it's to entertain, solve a problem, educate, or get your ideas across.

❑ Create a content style guide to keep all your social media stakeholders on the same page. Break down all the elements unique to your branding into individual segments. Ask yourself, is it clear enough that any new employees can quickly understand its contents?

❑ Practice writing short posts and calculating the length. How well can you stay within, say, a 100-character limit when composing a tweet?

❑ Open a new folder in one of your shared servers and start adding share-worthy images, videos, and presentations that would make great posts across your chosen platforms.

❑ Decide on a proper filing system for your content bank. Ensure all social media stakeholders have access to the necessary folders—including permissions to add and edit files within. Add a rule for consistent file name conventions in your style guide to maintain a clean and easy-access inventory.

❑ Make a 5x2 table like the one shown in Exhibit 5.1. Start by typing a different audience interest in each cell of row 1 in the order of the days of the week starting with Monday--ignore the weekend for the moment. Now format each of the cells in row 1 with a unique colour. Finally, add the types of content and various interests that fall under each daily category in row 2.

❑ Create a cheat sheet using graphics software of your choice. I made mine using PowerPoint. You may design your cheat sheet to look like mine, with unique colours to match the audience interest table and a box for every social media platform you plan to use. Or you can use your own unique style. Add the type of content you plan to post on each day and enter the approximate time the post will be published. Print and hang your cheat sheet where everyone can see it.

❑ Add Saturday and Sunday to your cheat sheet if you have the resources available. (This may need a slight design tweak in order to make it print-friendly.)

❑ Create an editorial calendar Excel spreadsheet. Feel free to copy my layout or design your own. Use your cheat sheet to help design the layout and make sure you include columns for date, time, platform, content type, text, and assets. Add any other relevant columns you wish such as post status and text length calculator.

❑ Examine the costs and features of social media management tools. Compare Hootsuite, Sprout Social, Sendible and any other application you may find or have heard of and select the most appropriate one for you.

❑ Make a list of sources you will use to find shareable content.

❑ Make a list of 20 social media influencers in your industry for Twitter and Instagram—if each one is in your list of selected social media platforms—that you can start following today.

☐ Expand your influencer list to include those users you plan to follow in the future (Remember, don't follow everyone at once!). Add new influencers to the list as and when you come across them on social media or within your social media management tool.

☐ Create your company's official social media policy document. Include straightforward guidelines for engaging with your followers and responding to comments and criticism.

☐ Decide on a salary for a social media specialist and a social media management tool based on your budget. These are your total costs.

☐ Devise a daily time management plan for your social media activity. Obviously, the more time you can spend on social media, the better your results will be.

☐ Plan your meeting with relevant stakeholders. Ensure you present justification behind your strategy and budget to accelerate understanding.

☐ Make a table of measurable and achievable KPIs. Determine when you are likely to achieve these results and how you will inform stakeholders.

❑ Familiarise yourself with analytics and reporting methods provided by your chosen social media management tool. Run test reports with your stakeholders to optimise the process before the first real report is implemented.

❑ Familiarise yourself with the paid-for options within LinkedIn, Facebook, and Twitter—not to start posting ads but more to answer any questions you may have and understand any features not covered in this chapter.

❑ If you plan to use social media marketing, add budgets for each platform in your list of costs as well as targets for ROI.

REFERENCES

- Abbott, W., Donaghey, J., Hare, J., & Hopkins, P. (2013). An Instagram Is Worth A Thousand Words: An Industry Panel And Audience Q&A. Library Hi Tech News, 30(7), 1-6.
- Abramovich, G. (March 10, 2014). 15 Mind-Blowing Stats About SlideShare.
- Ben-Moshe, T. (May 27, 2015). 7-Step Social Media Management Strategy For B2B Marketers.
- Bennett, S. (February 25, 2015). The Potential Of Social Media (For #B2B Marketers) [Infographic].
- Bodnar, K., & Cohen, J. L. (2011). B2B Social Media Book: Become A Marketing Superstar By Generating Leads With Blogging, LinkedIn, Twitter, Facebook, Email, And More. Hoboken, NJ, USA: John Wiley & Sons.
- Bonsón, E., & Bednárová, M. (2013). Corporate LinkedIn Practices Of Eurozone Companies. Online Information Review, 37(6), 969.
- Borgini, J. (August 30, 2013). Finding Your B2B Social Media Zen.
- Bosomworth, D. (March 26, 2012). 7 Reasons B2B Marketers Should Love SlideShare.
- Bradbury, D. (2014). Anonymity And Privacy: A Guide For The Perplexed. Network Security, 2014(10), 10-14.
- Braun, A. (June 4, 2015). B2B Marketing On LinkedIn: A Guide To Showcase Pages.
- Brooks, G., Heffner, A., & Henderson, D. (2014). A SWOT Analysis Of Competitive Knowledge From Social Media For A Small Start-Up Business. The Review of Business Information Systems (Online), 18(1), 23.
- Brouwer, B. (December 1, 2014). YouTube Now Sees 300 Hours Of Video Uploaded Every Minute.
- Buron, J. (November 6, 2013). How To: Use Twitter For B2B Lead Generation.
- Carah, N. (2014). Like, Comment, Share: Alcohol Brand Activity On Facebook. Deakin, ACT, Australia: Foundation for Alcohol Research & Education.
- Cooper, B., & Naatus, M. K. (2014). LinkedIn As A Learning Tool In Business Education. American Journal of Business Education (Online), 7(4), 299.
- Corliss, R. (February 21, 2012). How To Master Pinterest For B2B Marketing.

- Cowling, D. (January 1, 2015). Social Media Statistics Australia – December 2014.
- Dahl, D. (February 25, 2010). How To Develop A Business Growth Strategy.
- Deepa, N., & Deshmukh, S. (2013). Social Media Marketing: The Next Generation Of Business Engagement. International Journal of Management Research and Reviews, 3(2), 2461-2468.
- DeMers, J. (November 27, 2013). How To Run A Successful B2B Social Media Marketing Campaign.
- Doctor, V. (June 12, 2012). What Characters Can A Hashtag Include.
- Duggan, M., Ellison, N. B., Lampe, C., Lenhart, A. & Madden, M. (January 9, 2015). Social Media Update 2014.
- Edwards, J. (July 27, 2013). Mark Zuckerberg Has A 27-Year Plan For Adding Another 5 Billion Users On Facebook.
- Fell, C. (September 12, 2011). How B2B Firms Can Use LinkedIn For Effective Lead Generation.
- Fitzpatrick, P. (May 5, 2014). 12 Most Strategic Ways To Use Pinterest For Marketing.
- Frank, A. (December 4, 2014). B2B With Social Media: Which Network Should You Choose?
- Fryrear, A. (February 4, 2015). Is Pinterest A Waste Of Your B2B Marketing Dollar? Probably.
- Gilfoil, D. M., & Jobs, C. (2012). Return On Investment For Social Media: A Proposed Framework For Understanding, Implementing, And Measuring The Return. Journal of Business & Economics Research (Online), 10(11), 637.
- Godin, S. (December 22, 2008). What Is Viral Marketing?
- Green, E. (October 10, 2013). How SlideShare Is Revolutionizing B2B Content Marketing.
- Gulasy, L. (Jun 5, 2013). Social Media Marketing: 7 Tips For Better Business Twitter Bio Copy.
- Hootsuite. (September 4, 2014). 10 million Users, 10 million Stories.
- Jackson, R., Schneider, A., & Baum, N. (2011). Social Media Networking: YouTube And Search Engine Optimization. The Journal of Medical Practice Management: MPM, 26(4), 254-7.
- Järvinen, J., Tollinen, A., Karjaluoto, H., & Jayawardhena, C. (2012). Digital And Social Media Marketing Usage In B2B Industrial Section. Marketing Management Journal, 22(2), 102-117.
- Kim, H. (2014). The Role Of WOM And Dynamic Capability In B2B Transactions. Journal of Research in Interactive Marketing, 8(2), 84.
- King, D. L. (2015). Analytics, goals, and strategy for social media. Library Technology Reports, 51(1), 26-32, 2.
- Krashinsky, S., & Dingman, S. (March 29, 2012). Networking Site Pinterest In Battle Against Spammers. The Globe and Mail.
- Lacho, K. J., & Marinello, C. (2010). How Small Business Owners Can Use Social Networking To Promote Their Business. The Entrepreneurial Executive, 15, 127-133.
- Levitan, P. (April 30, 2014). Which Social Media Strategy Is Best For Advertising Agency New Business?
- Marsh, E. (September 4, 2014). 7 Serious Business And Legal Risks Of B2B Social Media Marketing.
- McQuail, D. (2010). McQuail's Mass Communication Theory. London; Los Angeles: SAGE.
- Messerschmidt, J. (May 19, 2015). A New Way To Discover Tweets.

- Mihalcea, A., & Savulescu, R. (2013). Social Networking Sites: Guidelines For Creating New Business Opportunities Through Facebook, Twitter And LinkedIn. Management Dynamics in the Knowledge Economy, 1(1), 39-53.
- Milbrath, S. (March 19, 2014). Are You Following the Social Media Rule of Thirds?
- Miller, W. (November 27, 2013). Videos Under Two Minutes Generate the Most YouTube Views.
- Narcisse, A. (January 15, 2014). Planning Your B2B Marketing Approach To Social Media: 3 Key Angles.
- Olenski, S. (February 28, 2013). SlideShare: The Quiet Giant Of Content Marketing.
- Overdrive Interactive (February 5, 2015). 2015 Social Media Map.
- Paranicas, P. (March 12, 2013). Hey, B2B: Grow Up And Get A Social Media Strategy, Will You?
- Patel, N. (February 20, 2015). The Ultimate Guide to Hashtags.
- Peterson, E. A. (2014). Business Strategies For Managing The Legal Risks Of Social Media. Journal of Management and Sustainability, 4(3), 96-101.
- Petrescu, P. (October 1, 2014). Google Organic Click-Through Rates In 2014.
- Pickard, T. (July 10, 2014). AdWords Vs. Bing Ads.
- Power, R. (January, 29, 2014). Creating A Social Media Strategy For B2B Audiences, Products And Services.
- Ray, M. (June 20, 2012). 7 Pinterest Tips For B2B Companies.
- Ritter, M. (August 13, 2014). Why You Need Google+ In Your B2B Marketing Strategy [Infographic].
- Robinson, A. (November 13, 2013). 6 Steps To Selling Your Marketing Idea Or Strategy To Your CEO.
- Safko, L. (2012). The Social Media Bible: Tactics, Tools, And Strategies For Business Success. Hoboken: John Wiley & Sons.
- Smith, O. (February 19, 2015). How Does Google Plus Fit into a B2B Social Media Marketing Strategy?
- Sobal, A. (July 14, 2014). 5 Reasons Why Your B2B Company Needs To Be Using Twitter.
- Social Dynamite (July, 2014). Best Times To Post On Social Media [Infographic].
- Solis, B. (July 5, 2013). The Conversation Prism (Version 4.0).
- Sood, S. C., & Pattinson, H. M. (2012). 21st Century Applicability Of The Interaction Model: Does Pervasiveness Of Social Media In B2B Marketing Increase Business Dependency On The Interaction Model? Journal Of Customer Behaviour, 11(2), 117-128.
- Sorokina, O. (Nov 6, 2014). Why You Need A Social Media Content Calendar For Your Business.
- Sorokina, O. (February 12, 2015). 9 B2B Social Media Marketing Tips For Social Media Managers.
- Steinway, M. (June 20, 2014). How To Select A B2B Social Media Management Tool.
- Taneja, S., & Toombs, L. (2014). Putting A Face On Small Businesses: Visibility, Viability, And Sustainability The Impact Of Social Media On Small Business Marketing. Academy of Marketing Studies Journal, 18(1), 249-260.
- Thomas, M. (October 22, 2014). How B2B Marketers Can Make The Most Of Social Media.
- Vaynerchuk, G. (2013). Jab, Jab, Jab, Right Hook: How To Tell Your Story In A Noisy Social World. Harper Collins.
- Walgrove, A. (February 4, 2015). 5 B2B Brands That Rock LinkedIn.

- Watts, D. J., Peretti, J., & Frumin, M. (2007). Viral Marketing For The Real World. Harvard Business School Pub.
- Westergaard, N. (August 27, 2012). 9 Tips For Building Your Brand With SlideShare.
- Wibowo, I. (March 28, 2013). Is Google+ Relevant To B2B Marketing?
- Wolfe, R. (March 20, 2013). Be Prepared To Manage Social Media Risks.
- Zappe, J. (October 29, 2013). 'Damning' Report Says Facebook Marketing Doesn't Work.

GLOSSARY

algorithm

a list of steps a computer follows in order to solve a problem, perform calculations or other problem-solving operations

ama

ask me anything (AMA) is an invitation for social media users to ask open questions during a live Q&A session

android

a mobile operating system designed primarily for touch screen mobile devices

app

a software program downloaded by a user on a mobile device to fulfil a particular purpose; also known as an application

audience
a group of people who view social media posts, blog articles, images, and online videos

authority
an individual having enough of a high level of expertise in their field to be respected or obeyed by other people

auto-populate
a software function that completes data in internet forms without a user's involvement

backlink
a hyperlink that links from its location on a third-party web page back to the website embedded in the link

best practice
social media procedures that are accepted or prescribed as being correct or most effective

blog
a web page that is regularly updated with articles written in an informal or conversational style

bookmark
a record of the address of a website to enable quick access in future

brand
a trademark or distinctive name identifying a product or organisation

brand awareness

the extent to which users recognise a brand's image, products or services

brand persona
a set of human characteristics which users can relate to that are attributed to a brand name

branded
the practice of assigning a brand name to something

call to action
an instruction to the audience to elicit an immediate and specific response

campaign
an organised business activity with the aim of achieving a certain goal

cheat sheet
a summarised version of research data or text typically placed on a single page and intended to aid memory

clout
influence or power and having the respect of one's peers

commentator
a person who discusses news within their chosen field

commenter
a user who comments on a social media post or blog article

company values
guiding principles that help to define how the company

and its employees should behave under different situation

competitor
an organisation engaged in commercial competition with others for the same audience

content
a form of communication posted online for audiences to engage with

content bank
a collection of previously created and approved posts to promote via social media profiles

content discovery
finding interesting and relevant content to share with an audience

content fatigue
a user's tendency to reduce their social media use after becoming overwhelmed by consuming so much content on social media sites

contingency plan
a plan devised to manage risk and follow alternative routes in the event of an unexpected outcome

colour palette
the defining set of colours used throughout a website, image or document

crisis management
the process by which a company deals with unfortunate events that threaten to harm the company

dashboard

a user interface that consolidates and displays profile information and performance in a single panel

digital marketing

a targeted and measurable marketing strategy to promote brands, products, and services using digital technologies

embed

to fix a graphic or video into a web page

emoticon

a digital icon or symbol that serves to represent a facial expression and convey the writer's emotions or clarify intent

file name convention

a set of agreed-upon rules used to assign names to files in a folder

follower

a social media user who has a strong interest or pays close attention to an individual or brand

freebie

a digital file, product or service that is provided or given free of charge

gif

files which contains a number of images or frames that are compressed to reduce file size and transfer time

Google AdWords

Google's online advertising program that allows advertisers place ads on Google Search results and partner websites

Google Analytics
a free analytics service offered by Google that tracks and reports website traffic

Google Search
the leading web search engine owned by Google

hashtag
a word, phrase or acronym preceded by a hash symbol (#) that is used on social media sites such as twitter to identify messages on a specific topic

home feed
a list of updates and news items on a user's own home page on a social media site

image optimisation
a graphic compression format that considers file size and image quality for publication on the web

infinite scroll
a website design practice in which content on the page continually loads as a user navigates down the page

influencer
social media users who have the power to produce effects because of their (real or perceived) authority, knowledge, and position

infographic

a graphic visual representation of information or data intended to present information quickly and clearly

intangible objectives

goals that cannot be measured by any scientific means such as brand awareness, brand sentiment, and relationship building

inventory

a complete listing of content on hand that is intended to be shared on social media

keyword

a word or phrase that describes a website, product or service and helps users find information when researching online

kpi

a key performance indicator (KPI) is a business metric used to measure performance against key business objectives

landing page

a web page which serves as the entry point for a visitor to a website or a particular section of a website

lead

an individual or organisation with the potential to express an interest in goods or services

lead form

the method of capturing information from individuals or organisations on a web page or landing page

lead generation
obtaining or receiving information from individuals or organisations for the purpose of selling them goods or services

like
a way of giving positive feedback and connecting with things a social media user cares about

link-shortening
a service that translates long URLs into abbreviated alternatives for the purpose of saving text space

LinkedInner
a user who connects with other users and consumes content on LinkedIn

mention
making a reference to another user's profile on social media platforms

meta description
a web page coding element that describes your page to search engines

microblogging
a web service that allows users to broadcast short messages to other users of the service

news feed (see home feed)

non-follower
any social media user who is not a follower of an individual or brand

objectives

a specific result that a business aims to achieve with available resources and within a set time frame

organic post

a social media post published a user without backing of paid distribution

pin

the method of posting digital images to the digital 'bulletin board' of Pinterest

post life

the period of time a social media post reaches its majority of views before audience numbers begin to drop off

professionals

a member of a profession or any person with expertise in a specified field

profile maintenance

maintaining regular upkeep of a social media profile such as updating account information and images

pseudo

having the appearance of something genuine but concealing the truth

purchase history

a record of online purchases which a user has made in the past

reach

the extent or range of a blog article or social media post

real estate

the area of a web page with which digital objects are embedded

resources

time, money, and other assets that can be drawn on by a person or business in order to market effectively

rule of thirds

a rule for social content that states that a third aims to promote the business, a third to share ideas and stories from thought leaders, and the final third to share personal interactions

scam website

a website that operates under false pretences in order to fraudulently obtain financial information, passwords, or other personal data

search engine

a program that searches for and identifies items in a database that correspond to keywords or characters specified by the searcher to find websites with relevant information

search rankings

the position at which a particular website appears in the results of a search engine query

seo

search engine optimisation (SEO) is

server
a computer which manages access to centralised resources or services in a network

set-and-forget
the method of installing or configuring something to run in the background without further user involvement

shareable
content worthy and able to be shared with other users over the internet

social media associate(s)
the actual person or people in charge of managing all of your social media activity.

social media etiquette
the code of behaviour guiding what is good, bad, right and wrong on social media

social media management tool
a tool that allows users to manage numerous social media accounts from a single dashboard

social media marketing
a method of advertising and sponsoring posts to help attract new social media users and generate sales

social media platform
websites that allow people and companies to interact and exchange information, pictures, and videos

social media presence

the visibility of a user or organisation on social media

social media specialist (see social media associate)

social recruiting
the method of recruiting candidates by using social media platforms to advertise positions

spamming
indiscriminately sending branded messages to a large numbers of Internet users

stakeholders
a person with an interest or concern in a company's activity and performance

thought leader
the informed opinion leaders and the go-to people in their field of expertise

timeline
a linear representation of important events in the order in which they occurred over a period of time

traction
measurable evidence of market demand for a brand, product or service

traffic
the amount of visitors a web site receives

transcription text
the textual representation of utterances in an audio or video file

trending

a social media post, blog article, video, or other digital content that is becoming increasingly popular

tweet

a posting made by a user on the social media platform Twitter

two-way interaction

marketing communication that allows organisations to interact with their target audience on social media

user engagement

the engagement of customers with a company or a brand on social media

user review

a review of a product or service made by a customer who purchased the product or service

viral

a social media post, blog article, video, or other digital content that is being circulated rapidly and widely from one internet user to another

virtual assistant

a person who provides professional administrative, technical, or other assistance to clients remotely from their home or other office

word of mouth

a form of promotion in which satisfied customers tell other people how much they like a business, product or service

ABOUT THE AUTHOR

Rich Walker has worked in both internet technology and digital marketing roles since 2005 and holds a Masters degree in Communication. Rich specialises in researching a business's current digital marketing activity and uncovering opportunities to improve lead generation with modest increases in resources. In 2015, Rich worked with two Australian B2B companies and a major international travel organisation to develop their marketing strategies for the digital sphere, and looks forward to more consulting gigs in the future.

Rich also has a strong analytical background and ability to attack problems logically, which he owes to his Honours Bachelors degree in Mathematics. Rich has submitted two research papers on social media to respected academic journals and writes about several topics within the realm of digital marketing on his blog.

If you found any part of this book helpful, please leave a candid review on Amazon.

Thank you,
Rich

Printed in Great Britain
by Amazon